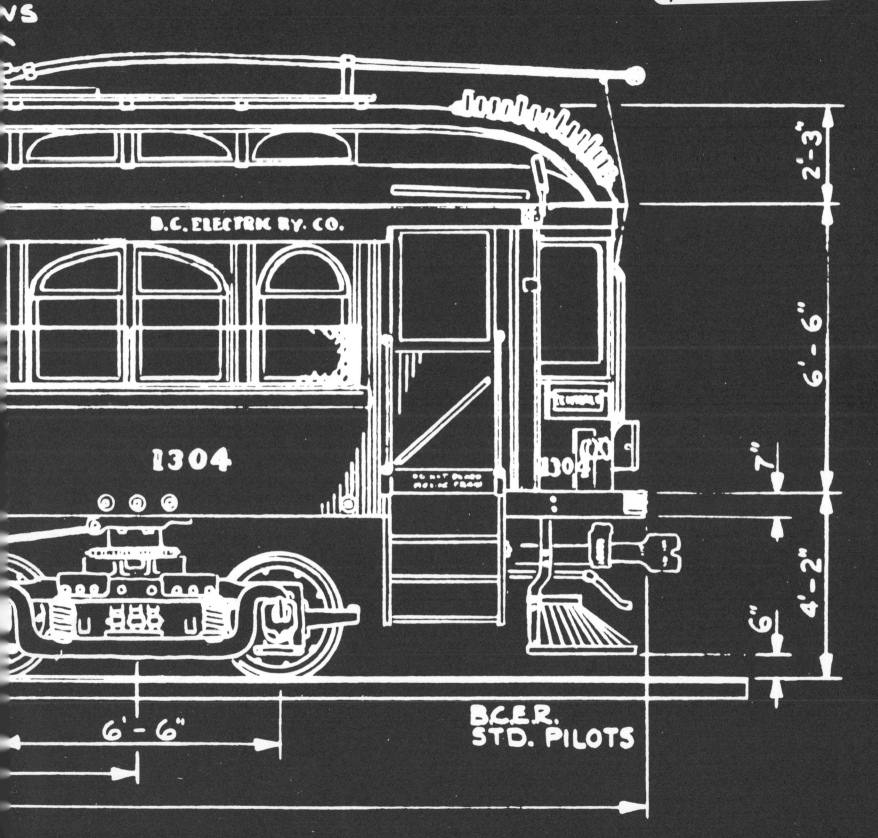

B.C. ELECTRIC RY. CO.

1304

BCER.
STD. PILOTS

6' - 6"

2'-3"

6'-6"

7"

4'-2"

6"

TRANSIT IN BRITISH COLUMBIA
THE FIRST HUNDRED YEARS

One of Vancouver's early streetcars, Car 53 survived as a salt car for several years after it retired from regular service. In 1955 it was presented to the PNE, where it was put on public display. Today it sits inside a restaurant in Vancouver's Gastown.

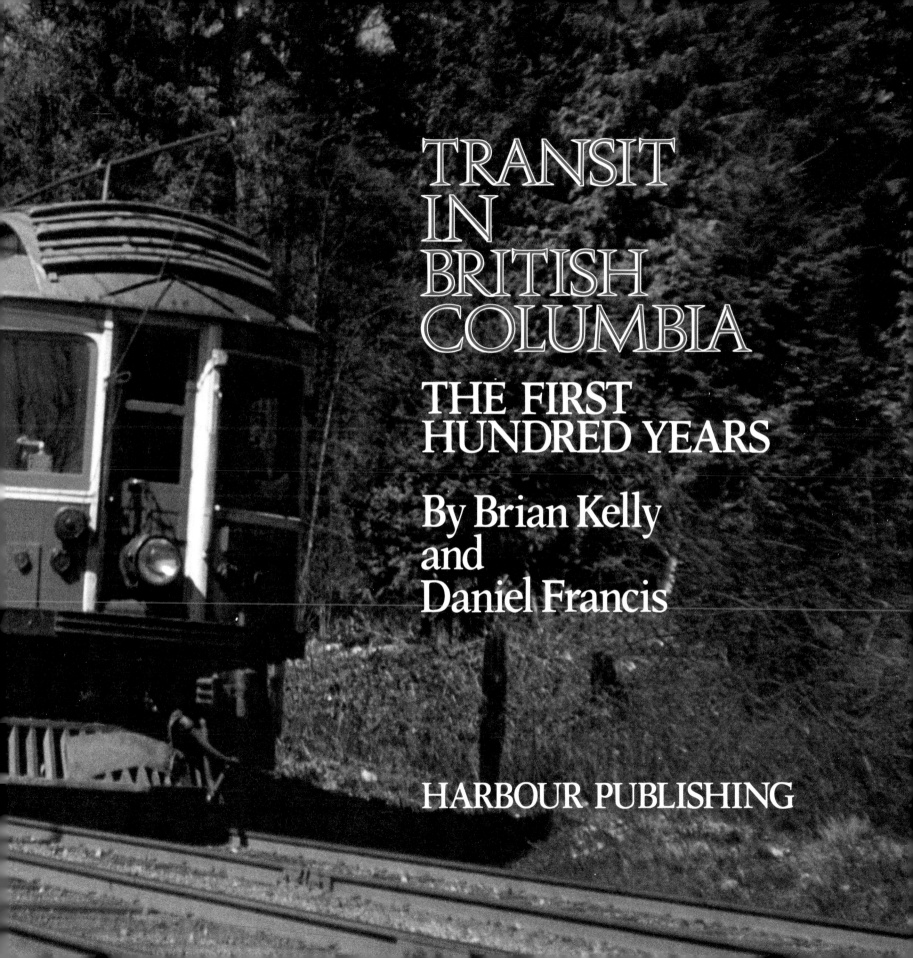

TRANSIT IN BRITISH COLUMBIA

THE FIRST HUNDRED YEARS

By Brian Kelly
and
Daniel Francis

Harbour Publishing

Design by Roger Handling
Maps by Theresa Magee
Printed and bound in Hong Kong by Colorcraft

HARBOUR PUBLISHING CO. LTD.
Box 219
Madeira Park, BC V0N 2H0

Canadian Cataloguing in Publication Data

Kelly, Brian, 1947–
    Transit in British Columbia

ISBN 1-55017-021-X
    1. Local transit—British Columbia—
History. I. Title.
HE311.C32B754 1990   388.4′09711   C90-091112-3

CONTENTS

◄
April 29, 1926. Street-car 346 heads east on Cordova Street towards Carrall in downtown Vancouver. Many of the buildings in the photograph still stand today. Compare this photograph to the one on page 16, taken at the same spot 35 years earlier.

I know that many people tend to overlook special occasions such as anniversaries, birthdays and centennials, but I always look upon them as useful opportunities to pause and reflect on past accomplishments and to develop plans for the future. The year 1990 marks a very special anniversary. It was exactly 100 years ago that the first electric street railways opened for business in Victoria and Vancouver, inaugurating the history of public transit in British Columbia.

The centenary of public transit allows us to acknowledge the great changes and improvements that have occurred over the past 100 years. Trundling along at speeds up to 10 kilometres per hour, the earliest wooden streetcars carried passengers from one end of town to the other for a fare of just one nickel. In time, elegant steel cars replaced the rickety four-wheelers. Then came motor buses and trolley coaches and eventually, the ultramodern SkyTrain. Today, a century after it all began, more than 130 million passengers use public transit in the province each year, and transit plays an important role in the social and economic development of communities throughout the province.

Transit in British Columbia: The First Hundred Years is an illustrated history of transit in the province, published to mark the centennial. The book describes the transit vehicles, and pays tribute to the people who operated them. It traces the evolution of transit from the pioneer companies which laid the first streetcar tracks, to the BC Electric Company, which for so many years owned the system, to the Metro Transit Operating Company and finally to BC Transit, the Crown corporation which now administers transit in the province. The history is illustrated with a large selection of photographs both old and new, many of them never before seen in print.

Life in our towns and cities has changed a lot in the past hundred years, but one thing that has not changed is the need for inexpensive, efficient forms of public transportation. Initially, this need was met by a few streetcars and a handful of employees. Today it is met by a much larger workforce and the latest in modern technology. *Transit in British Columbia* presents a colourful review of these changes in pictures and words. It is dedicated to all the men and women who have worked so hard over the years to keep British Columbians "on the move."

R. Dennis Cooney,
Chairperson,
BC Transit Centennial Committee

◄
A streetcar rounds the loop at Kitsilano Beach, one of the most popular recreation spots in Vancouver.

My mother often told me that she frequently found me, as a small boy, at the bus loop a few blocks from our home in Belfast, Northern Ireland, watching the big red and cream double-decker trolley buses turning around to journey back downtown. They started an interest in transportation that remains and fascinates me to this very day.

When we arrived in Vancouver, the last of the BC Electric's vast streetcar and interurban network was all but gone. My memories are vivid of catching the ''tram'' downtown from our home at Collingwood East, and transferring to a PCC for a ride out East Hastings to the exhibition or some other destination.

The day arrived, years later, when I began a career in transit that I enjoy to the fullest each day, and a career that has been very good to me. I spent many hours talking to senior employees about the earlier days, and I am eternally grateful to them for passing on to me, not only their stories, but their keepsakes in the form of old transfers, tickets, photos and more. Not too long into my work with what was then BC Hydro Transit, I determined to research the complete story of the system and write it down, before the memories of those early days were gone, never to be recaptured.

The result of this determination, some 15 years later, is a collection of photographs, stories, and artifacts, and three volumes of a history I have written called *Rails to Rubber* after the BC Electric's own program of the late 1940s. The first volume, *The Streetcars*, will be released later this year, with volume two, *The Interurbans*, and volume three, *The Buses and Trolleys*, to follow soon after. It is my hope that these books will bring delight not only to those interested in the history of our cities and our transit systems, but also to the people who worked "on the job,'' or who rode the big red and cream trams, streetcars and buses, and remember them well.

1990 is centennial year at BC Transit, and it was with excitement I accepted the honour and privilege of putting together a condensed version of my books and photographs to be published as part of the centennial celebrations. The result is *Transit in British Columbia: The First Hundred Years.*

Space does not permit me to thank all the transportation enthusiasts, the BC Electric enthusiasts, the retirees, the archives and museum curators, and the dozens of others who came forward with pieces of the puzzle. But I would be very remiss in not thanking the hard-working BC Transit Centennial Committee for their support in this project, especially our committee chairperson, Dennis Cooney, and fellow member of the book sub-committee, Diane Gendron. Thanks also to Howard White and Roger Handling of Harbour Publishing for bringing the book to reality. And a special thanks to Dan Francis, who not only edited my work, but wrote the modern times segment himself.

A very special thanks must go to our senior management, board members, and especially our Chairman Stu Hodgson, himself a real BC Electric fan for many years. Without this support from the top, the whole centennial celebration, not to mention this book, would have been much more difficult, if not impossible.

Last but not least, I thank my wife Wendy, who has supported me enthusiastically all the way.

I had a lot of fun working on this book. I hope you have as much fun reading it.

Brian Kelly

◄
Ono of tho original Vancouver streetcars boards passengers at Denman and Davie in 1904. Since inaugurating the system 14 years earlier, the car has added closed-in vestibules, lifeguards, advertisements, and an illuminated roof destination sign. The large letter F over the headlight indicates that the car's ultimate destination is Fairview. It must be summertime, since the motorman on the right is wearing his cooler, summer cap.

CHAPTER ONE

STREET RAILWAYS

Public transit arrived in British Columbia on Saturday afternoon, February 22, 1890. The site was Victoria, the provincial capital. Not yet 50 years old, Victoria was a former fur-trade post that had prospered as a fishing and sealing port, and as a jumping-off point for prospectors and loggers who arrived to make their fortunes in the new land. Not all pioneers were miners and lumberjacks, however. Many were businessmen, dedicated to the growth and development of their adopted city. Among them were the founders of Victoria's street railway.

A crowd of expectant well-wishers gathered that afternoon to witness the first running of an electric streetcar system west of Ontario. Champagne corks popped, the crowd sang *God Save the Queen*, and Lieutenant-Governor Hugh Nelson declared the line officially open. With that, Car 1, bedecked with flags and streamers and loaded with dignitaries, set off down Store Street.

◄
One of Victoria's original streetcars stops on Government Street at Fort to take on passengers. The car is heading for Beacon Hill Park.

Saturday, February 22, 1890. Lieutenant Governor Hugh Nelson, in the centre of the platform on Car 1, doffs his hat to the crowd and a few moments later starts the car forward, ushering electric transportation into Western Canada.

David William Higgins, editor of the Victoria Colonist and founder of the National Electric Tramway and Lighting Company, operators of the first electric streetcars in Western Canada. Originally from the Maritimes, he joined the gold rush to BC in 1858, later settling in Victoria where his original home at 1501 Fort Street has been restored and is open to the public. Higgins was the first president of the Tramway Company, serving until he resigned at the end of 1893.

After the initial run, the system opened to the riding public. Over 4000 people paid the nickel fare that allowed them to race back and forth at speeds up to 15 kilometres an hour. Businesses along the way proudly advertised that ''cars pass the door.'' At night the cars were illuminated, reported the local newspaper, and ''dashed through the streets in busy metropolitan style: the admiration of all lovers of enterprise, convenience and progress.'' It was, as Premier John Robson proudly declared, ''a new era in the progress of Victoria.''

Throughout the world, street railways were in their infancy, but they were fast becoming a vital element in the growth of modern cities. Large centres in eastern Canada introduced horse-drawn streetcars in the 1860s, and horses remained the motive power for several years. But the size and speed of horse-powered railways were limited; plus, the animals suffered horribly from the exhausting work. By the 1880s engineers were perfecting electric railways, using overhead wires and trolley poles. In 1886 Windsor, Ontario, installed the first electric street railway line in Canada, followed closely by St. Catharines.

The driving force behind British Columbia's first electric railway was David William Higgins, editor of the Victoria *Colonist* newspaper. Receiving a charter from the city, Higgins and his associates organized the National Electric Tramway and Lighting Company. With capital of $250,000, a huge amount of money for the time, the new company determined to provide street lighting, domestic and industrial power, and a street railway. It began laying track in the summer of 1889.

Rails came from Belgium; electrical equipment from the firm of Thomson-Houston, the forerunner of General Electric; and the Ontario car builder Patterson and Corbin supplied the four original cars. And what magnificent cars they were: four wheelers with 16-foot bodies made of cherrywood and canvas, resplendent with brass trim. Each had room for 24 passengers, sitting on two benches running lengthwise down the car. Stoves kept the interior warm, while coal oil headlamps showed the way at night. The conductor and the motorman, or ''motineer'' as he was called, stood out on open platforms, front and rear. In bad weather the poor chaps got so cold and wet that either one was permitted to operate the car if the other wanted to jog alongside to keep warm.

The original system, opened with such pride on February 22, consisted of two routes along nine kilometres of track. Success was immediate, and in little more than a year the system virtually doubled in size. Streetcars now ran out the Oak Bay Line to Windsor Park, home of the city's lacrosse team, while in the opposite direction the first ''interborough'' line travelled out to Esquimalt, site of the Royal Navy dockyard. These streetcars frequently were packed with sailors, and a good thing too. Trackwork to Esquimalt was poor and derailments were frequent, but it hardly took a minute for a group of sailors to hop off, lift the car back onto the track, and carry on as though nothing had happened.

Almost at the end of the line, a streetcar bound for Esquimalt crosses a section of wooden trestle near Signal Hill about 1892. The church in the background, St. Paul's, eventually moved half a dozen blocks closer to Victoria because its stained glass windows shattered every time naval vessels at Esquimalt fired their heavy guns.

Car 2 is off the rails on its way to Esquimalt. Crew and passengers are probably waiting for the next group of sailors to come by and help them hoist the car back onto the track.

Vancouver (Gastown) 1884 - B.C.

In the meantime, Vancouver, not content to rest in Victoria's shadow, was building a street railway of its own. Since the devastating fire of 1886, Vancouver had grown in leaps and bounds. Within five years the population grew to 15,000 people. Streets were laid out, and development spread south from the swampy shores of Burrard Inlet. The need for a system of public transportation grew more pressing.

Several promoters submitted plans to city council and finally on April 6, 1889, the Vancouver Street Railway was incorporated and began laying track down Granville Street. Originally the directors of the company intended to use horse-drawn rail cars, but Henry McKee, a lawyer from Omaha with a lot of experience with American street railways, persuaded them to opt for electricity instead.

The townsite of Granville in 1884, huddled along the shores of Burrard Inlet. On the extreme left is the Sunnyside Hotel. Adjoining it on the right are a butcher shop, the two-storey Granville Hotel, and other homes and shops. Two years later this pioneer settlement became the city of Vancouver.

Looking due north on Westminster Avenue, now Main Street, at Powell in Vancouver in the summer of 1889. Workers are laying the original streetcar track in a "wye" formation so that cars can swing either west into the city centre or east out to the sugar refinery.

It is the summer of 1894, and a Victoria streetcar coming in from Spring Ridge turns off Yates onto Government Street. In the background is the Bismark Hotel, long a familiar landmark in the capital.

David Oppenheimer, the second mayor of Vancouver. Born in Germany, he arrived in BC in 1860. Along with his brother Isaac, he established a successful grocery business in Victoria, later moving to Vancouver where he was involved in many development schemes. He was a shareholder in the Vancouver Electric Illuminating Company, which later became part of the Vancouver Electric Railway and Light Company, and president of the Westminster and Vancouver Tramway Company. Ill health forced Oppenheimer to leave politics in 1891; he died at the end of 1897.

Dominion Day, July 1, 1890. Vancouver's streetcar system has been in operation for five days. Car 14 is leading the parade down Cordova Street through the city's main business district towards Carrall. The same scene, 35 years later, is on page 2.

This decision caused a delay while the company sold its horses and stable, strung trolley wire and purchased six cars from the American builder, John Stephenson. The streetcar company then merged with the local illuminating company to create the Vancouver Electric Railway and Light Company, with Mayor David Oppenheimer as director.

On June 26, 1890, just four months after Victoria, Vancouver was ready to open its new transit system. Hundreds of curious onlookers crowded the sidewalks as motorman Aubrey Elliott and conductor Dugald Carmichael took Car 14 out of the car house on Barnard Street and away down Westminster Avenue, now Main Street, on a trial run. Then the directors of the company pressed all the cars into service and everyone rode free for the rest of the day. Two days later the entire system, all 9.6 kilometres of it, opened for regular service at five cents a ride.

The Vancouver streetcars resembled Victoria's—small four-wheelers with bench seats and open platforms. Two were smaller still, having been designed as trailers, then later converted to powered cars. Instead of numbering the cars starting at one, the company numbered them 10 to 15 in an attempt to impress visitors with the size of Vancouver's transit system.

The streetcar company immediately began planning for expansion and the next year, 1891, the system doubled in size. Using the new Granville Street Bridge, the line crossed False Creek to the top of the Fairview Heights, where it turned east through an opening in the forest that would one day be Broadway. Reaching Westminster, streetcars turned north to link up with the original line.

By this time the third pioneer, the Westminster and Vancouver Tramway Company, had inaugurated streetcar service in New Westminster, and was constructing North America's first true electric interurban line between Vancouver and the Royal City. But before the three street railways got firmly established, British Columbia plunged into a recession. The growth projected for the

Four of Vancouver's original streetcars pose proudly in front of the car barn on Barnard Street (now Union Street), just west of Main late in 1890. Note the bell-shaped clerestory roof, a trademark of all cars built by John Stephenson. The powerhouse, with its large chimney, stands in the background.

In Victoria, one of the original trailers, now converted to a regular open-sided, or "toastrack"-style car.

Francis S. Barnard was a pioneer of public transit in Victoria. In 1885 he began the capital's first omnibus service, running large, horse-drawn wagons on three routes through the city. He was president of the Consolidated Railway Company that operated the street railways in Victoria, Vancouver and New Westminster, and became the first managing director of the BC Electric Company when it was created in 1897. From 1888 to 1896 he was a Conservative member of parliament. Knighted in 1918, he served as lieutenant governor of the province from 1914 to 1919.

1890s did not materialize. Settlers did not appear in large numbers. The expected development did not occur along Victoria's Esquimalt line and out Vancouver's Fairview line. Fares failed to cover operating expenses, and the directors of the Vancouver system bemoaned the fact that "profits from the sale of electricity have to subsidize the transit system."

Unable to raise enough capital at home, the street railway companies sought help in England. By 1895 the English firm of Sperling and Company had taken over financial control of the Victoria system. Meanwhile, another English company, Yorkshire Guarantee and Loan, joined the Bank of British Columbia to reorganize the Vancouver and New Westminster systems into one company, the Consolidated Railway and Light Company.

Consolidated's president was a prominent British Columbia businessman, and future lieutenant governor, Francis S. Barnard. Sperling and Company sent a young representative, Robert Horne-Payne, out from London to look after its interests. The two men happened to meet in the tiny mining town of Nelson and fell to discussing their mutual interest, street railways. A plan was devised to raise money for a company that would control all the power, light and street railway systems in Victoria, Vancouver and New Westminster. On May 1, 1896, Barnard and Horne-Payne united the province's

► Kingsway at Central Park, as it was in 1891, looking west down the hill to Joyce Road. The car in the foreground is a New Westminster city streetcar; the other is an interurban tram.

three transit systems for the first time, as the Consolidated Railway Company.

The future looked promising for the new company. The Victoria streetcar system had expanded to sixteen cars. In Vancouver, a new line reached down Robson Street to the fashionable West End. Advertising appeared on the cars for the first time, and busy lines were double-tracked so that cars could pass freely without waiting at sidings. The recession showed signs of lifting. Then tragedy struck.

On May 26, 1896, Victoria Day, the Royal Navy planned a sail past and mock battle off Esquimalt to celebrate the Queen's birthday. Almost the entire city of Victoria journeyed out to see the display, most of them by streetcar. The company called in off-duty crews and pressed every car it could muster into service.

The line to Esquimalt crossed the waters of the Gorge on the Point Ellice Bridge. All morning, crowded streetcar after crowded streetcar passed over it. At ten minutes to two in the afternoon, Car 16, one of the largest vehicles in the fleet, crammed with 143 passengers, trundled out onto the bridge. It reached the middle of the span when witnesses heard a loud cracking sound. The deck dropped several centimetres, and then with a tremendous roar the entire structure collapsed into the water. Car 16 seemed to ride the rails for a few horrible seconds while the roadway fell away beneath it, then it too plunged into the harbour, coming to rest on the bottom skewered through by broken timbers from the bridge.

Doctors, policemen, navy divers and other rescuers rushed to the scene. The stately home of Captain William Grant, near the east end of the bridge, became a makeshift hospital and morgue as body after body was pulled from the water and laid out on the lawns. In all, 55 persons died, many of them small children. It is still the worst accident in Canadian transit history. Most of the dead were passengers on Car 16, but not all. One victim was riding his bicycle across the bridge when it collapsed. Another was a passenger in an open buggy that went down in the wreckage. There was scarcely a family in Victoria that was not touched by the disaster.

Francis Barnard and Robert Horne-Payne barely missed being victims of the tragedy themselves. Visiting from England, Horne-Payne crossed the bridge with his host, Barnard, on their way to Esquimalt just moments before the collapse. The two men rushed back and took part in rescue efforts.

But there was no rescuing their company. Fearing lawsuits, investors pulled out their money. Passengers stopped riding streetcars, especially across bridges, and the inquest into the accident dragged on and on. Ultimately the city was blamed for not maintaining the bridge, but the Consolidated Railway went bankrupt just the same.

Undeterred, Barnard and Horne-Payne set about raising capital in England for another street railway company. Within a year, they had succeeded, and on April 15, 1897, the two promoters launched a new company to run the electric utilities, lighting and streetcars in the province. Its name: the British Columbia Electric Railway Company.

Johannes Buntzen, secretary of the Consolidated Railway and Light Company and first general manager of the BC Electric Railway. Under his management, the streetcars and interurbans experienced their greatest growth. He retired as general manager in 1905 and returned to live in his native Denmark, but he remained a member of the BCER board of directors. Buntzen died in 1922.

The BC Electric took control of public transit just as the province was emerging from its recession. Under the supervision of General Manager Johannes Buntzen, the company embarked on a period of expansion that lasted right up to the outbreak of the First World War.

In Victoria, Buntzen promoted a young man named Albert Toller Goward manager for the company. Goward had started work with the old Consolidated Company, and would work for 50 years, one of the longest careers in company history. He became the personification of the BCER on Vancouver Island.

Under Goward's direction, the company built a new car barn on Pembroke Street, designed by architect Francis Rattenbury, famous for his work on the legislature build-

The BC Electric Railway's first Vancouver office, on Cordova Street, in the summer of 1897. The company is so new that lettering for the old Consolidated Railway can still be seen on the window.

The Pembroke Street car barn in Victoria, ca. 1925. The building is still standing, the only surviving streetcar barn from the BCER era.

ings and later the Empress Hotel. In the summer of 1905 a new line opened off the Esquimalt Road out to Gorge Park. Operated by the BCER, the park developed into a major attraction, ''a fairyland of sylvan beauty'' as the *Colonist* called it, featuring dancing, roller skating, water sports, tea houses and manicured gardens.

New lines also opened to the south of the city centre out to the cemetery at Ross Bay, and east across the peninsula to the expanding residential neighbourhoods of Oak Bay. By 1914 the Victoria system had 50 streetcars operating along close to 100 kilometres of track.

The pre-war years saw expansion in New Westminster as well, but it was in Vancouver, and the neighbouring municipalities of Point Grey and South Vancouver, that the company enjoyed a tremendous growth in service. By 1905 streetcars ran through the West End to Stanley Park, south down Main Street as far as 33rd Avenue, and west to Greer's Beach, now Kitsilano, where a beach house and dance hall attracted bathers on warm summer days.

Albert Toller Goward was involved with transit on Vancouver Island from 1891 until his retirement in 1945.

In 1906, Car 20, recently rebuilt as a closed car, rounds the corner off Fort Street and heads north up Government in downtown Victoria.

Victoria's observation car at Gorge Park. On this particular day the car is jammed with sightseers, but in general the Victoria observation car was not popular with the public and in 1919 the company transferred it to Vancouver.

Car 36 at the entrance to Stanley Park in 1902. It was one of the original Brill cars from the Westminster and Vancouver Tramway, rebuilt for city streetcar service.

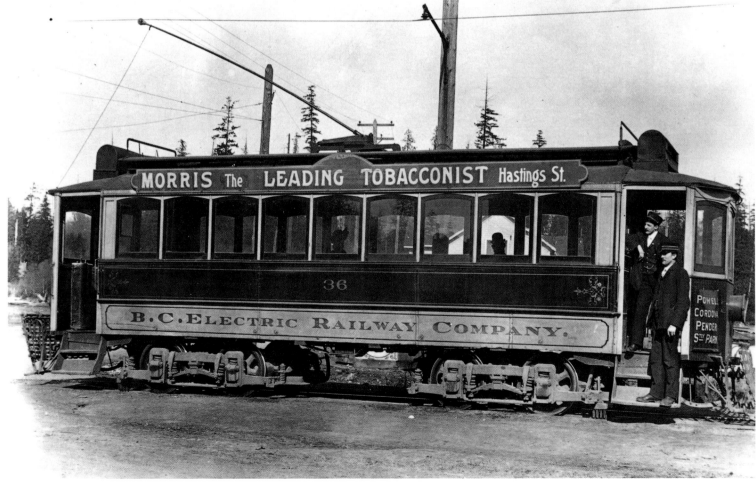

The treadle door opened automatically when a passenger stepped on it. Note the Cleveland farebox and manual brake wheel in this photograph of a streetcar interior.

STREETCARS IN THE KOOTENAYS

The BC Electric was not the only transit company in the province. On December 21, 1899, the city of Nelson inaugurated its own street railway system, owned and operated by the Nelson Electric Tramway Company. A derailment two days later, which cost a motorman his arm, delayed the start of regular revenue service to December 27.

The Nelson system was a proud achievement for such a small city. Boasting two streetcars (seen in the photograph above) and about eight kilometres of track, the railway was dubbed "the smallest streetcar system in the British Empire."

It rarely turned a profit. Financial problems caused a suspension of service for several weeks in 1904 and the city agreed to lease the line for $5 a year. But problems continued. After a fire in 1908, service was not restored for two years.

In 1914 the city bought the system and ran it as the first publicly-owned street railway in the province. Gas buses forced the electric cars into retirement in 1949, but one of the original old vehicles has been restored.

Looking north up Westminster Avenue (Main Street) from Broadway in Vancouver in 1907. The Mount Pleasant Methodist Church is visible behind the streetcar on the left.

Between 1900 and 1910 the population of Vancouver almost quadrupled, fulfilling the prediction in the local slogan: "By 1910, Vancouver then, will have 100,000 men." All these newcomers needed somewhere to live, and the city experienced a construction boom. The streetcars spearheaded the development by spreading out in all directions from the downtown. New homes quickly followed. On the eve of the war, the Vancouver fleet numbered 232 cars.

One of the best remembered of the new routes was the Oak Street Line, nicknamed the "Toonerville Trolley" after a popular cartoon of the era. Extending down Oak Street all the way to Marpole, the line was single track beyond 16th Avenue and right to the end used the old-fashioned "staff" system. The staff was a wooden bar kept at the passing tracks built at intervals along the single-track line. As one car came down the line, the motorman leaned out and passed the staff to the motorman of the car waiting on the passing track. Only the car with the staff was allowed to venture out onto the main line; other cars had to wait.

As the system grew, the BCER could not get enough new cars to meet its needs, especially being on the west coast and so far

►
The BCER line crew used this horse-drawn wagon to string and repair trolley wire in Vancouver.

Rochfort Henry Sperling, general manager of the BC Electric from 1905 to 1913. Son of a partner in Sperling and Company, he came out from England in 1898 as superintendent of the Goldstream hydroelectric plant. As general manager, he presided over a busy period of expansion for the street railways. After leaving Canada, he returned to England to join the board of the BCER.

away from the major manufacturers. As a result, the company took a rather bold step and began to build its own cars. At the foot of the 12th Street hill in New Westminster, it acquired a piece of property and put up a new car barn and large factory. Thomas Driscoll was hired as the master builder, and on April 2, 1903, he delivered his first finished products, Cars 50 and 52 for Vancouver, small four wheelers painted green and cream.

Within a couple of years the company made arrangements with J.G. Brill, one of the largest streetcar builders, to manufacture cars on the Brill design with Brill running gear at its New Westminster plant. These were larger, double-truck vehicles in the Narraganset or curved-side style, and set the pattern for virtually every streetcar the company built over the next several years. The double-truck cars made their first appearance

The 12th Street car barns and factory in New Westminster. The BC Electric built this facility in 1902 when it realized that other manufacturers could not meet its growing demand for new streetcars.

One of the Narraganset-style cars under construction at the BC Electric's New Westminster factory. The factory was located at the foot of 12th Street near what is now Stewardson Way.

on the Kitsilano line and soon were seeing duty on all the lines in Vancouver, Victoria and New Westminster. The little four wheelers were scrapped, or converted to work cars; the last one ran in regular passenger service on the eve of World War One.

The fourth, and smallest, streetcar system in the BCER network was in North Vancouver where residents petitioned the company to start a service. Power lines were strung across the Second Narrows on tall masts, some light rail was rescued from the scrap heap, and using a trio of four wheelers due for retirement, public transit came to North Vancouver on Labour Day, September 3, 1906.

At the time, a ferry system connected the North Shore to downtown Vancouver. The forerunner of today's SeaBus, the ferry ran

Two streetcars await the arrival of the ferry at the foot of Lonsdale Avenue in North Vancouver ca. 1910.

One of the Narragansets in operation in the summer of 1908, heading west on Hastings at Cambie in downtown Vancouver. At that time the streetcars were painted green, with white trim and red-bordered gold lettering along both upper window sashes. The tin ''wing signs'' hanging by the front door were forerunners of the modern destination signs.

Trackman Dominic Albanese, working with his grease bucket and paddle, is greasing the rails so that streetcar wheels will not squeal, bind, or even derail.

HARD LUCK ON THE NORTH SHORE

Jack Kelly was conductor on board the first streetcar to make a run up Lonsdale Avenue in North Vancouver in September 1906. On the trip up, everything worked perfectly. But on the way back down the steep incline, flag-draped Car 25 lost its brakes and came skidding into the next car waiting at the bottom. Fortunately no one was injured so, with the damage covered by more flags and bunting, the festivities continued.

The following January, the BCER arranged to deliver a flatcar loaded with motors to the Diplock Mills near 17th Street and Lonsdale. A barge carried the flatcar by water to the foot of Lonsdale where it coupled onto the little North Vancouver work car for the long haul up the hill. Streetcar 25 came along behind to push, and Jack Kelly supervised the operation.

The train got as far as 3rd Street, at which point the weight of the flatcar overcame the power of the work car and back down the hill it came, pushing the poor streetcar ahead of it. With everyone jumping for their lives, the cars plunged off the end of the track into the water. Only the work car survived, badly damaged, and Jack Kelly had another wild ride down Lonsdale to talk about.

Things went pretty smoothly for Jack for the next couple of years. Then, one August afternoon in 1909, he was at the controls of Car 62 as it headed down Lonsdale to meet the 4 p.m. ferry from Vancouver. Once again the brakes failed. With 15 passengers screaming in fright, including the wife of the mayor of North Vancouver, the car careened down the hill and off the end of the dock. Along with a couple of passengers, Kelly leaped from the car, breaking his leg. The rest were fished safely out of the harbour. In the photograph above, Car 62 lies forlornly on its side in the water after the accident.

That was enough for Motorman Kelly. He put in an immediate request to come off the Lonsdale run, a request the company was happy to approve.

FERRY WHARF NORTH VANCOUVER B.C.

Looking down Lonsdale Avenue in North Vancouver on a busy Dominion Day holiday, ca. 1908. The ferry St. George is boarding passengers at the slip, while another ferry, the Surrey, is setting off across the harbour. Ferry passengers arriving from Vancouver found streetcars from all three North Shore routes waiting at the foot of the hill.

A car on the Lynn Valley line in North Vancouver passes the area's general store on Mountain Highway, ca. 1912.

from Carrall Street across the inlet to the foot of Lonsdale Avenue. The new streetcar line began at the ferry wharf. Ascending Lonsdale through the heart of the city's business district, the line originally stopped at 12th Street. Eventually, it extended up the hillside as far as Windsor Avenue. The car barn was located at 3rd Street and St. David's next to an electrical substation, still the site of the substation and bus garage today.

Lonsdale was known as the ''north-south line.'' By December 1906, it was joined by an ''east-west line'' running across the municipality from Queensbury Avenue to the vicinity of Keith Road and Marine Drive. In time the North Vancouver service grew to 11 cars and three routes: one up Lonsdale, one out Lynn Valley Road and the third running west toward the Capilano Canyon.

In 1914, the First World War broke out. While Canadians flocked overseas to fight the foreign enemy, the BCER faced an enemy of its own on the home front. For the first time competition appeared, in the form

In September 1914, passengers cling to the back platform of a crowded streetcar in downtown Vancouver.

William George Murrin, former superintendent of the London United Tramways, rose through the ranks of the BCER to become president of the company in 1929. He retired in 1946, though he remained on the board of directors.

of the jitney. A jitney was simply a privately-owned automobile, usually a Model T Ford, which motored down the street picking up passengers ahead of the streetcar. By 1916 the BCER counted close to 500 of these interlopers running during rush hour, compared to 160 streetcars. Many displayed signs reading ''Dunbar—5 cents,'' or ''Fairview—5 cents.'' When some dropped their fares to four cents, the electric company's howls of outrage grew even louder.

The BCER lobbied city and provincial governments to ban the jitneys. It took out advertising in the newspapers begging passengers to remain faithful to the streetcars. It slashed fares, and improved service. Matters came to a head in 1917 when frustrated transit workers went on strike. The province at last responded with an official inquiry, and in 1918 civic officials banned the jitneys.

The end of the war inaugurated a time of change for the streetcars. In July 1918, the company raised car fares to six cents, the first increase in the 28-year history of the system. In 1921 Victoria introduced the one-man car, followed by New Westminster and parts of Vancouver. Lonsdale in North Vancouver and the busier Vancouver routes continued to use two-man cars. Instead of a motorman and conductor, the new cars had a single operator. To indicate whether passengers should board by the front doors and pay the operator, or by the rear doors and pay the conductor, the one-man cars were painted with a large X across the front. Later, the insignia was filled in to give the cars a ''bow-tie'' look.

Victoria also ordered new lightweight, four-wheel cars called Birneys after their designer, Charles Birney. The school children were thrilled to discover that if they crowded to the back of the car and bounced up and down the little four wheeler would bounce off the track, making all on board late for school. The operators nicknamed them ''Kangaroos.''

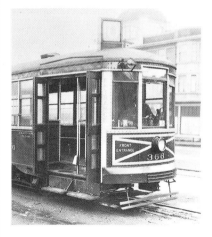

The X painted across the front of a streetcar indicated that it was a one-man car and that passengers should board at the front and pay their fare to the operator.

One of Vancouver's dwindling fleet of streetcars at 25th Avenue and Oak Street in May, 1951.

FARE, PLEASE!
For the first 28 years of service, streetcars in Vancouver charged a nickel for a ride. Conductors collected the fare in a leather-bound brass box with a jug handle, known as "the coffee pot." At first conductors walked up and down the aisle taking the fare. In 1909 the first Pay As You Enter cars were introduced; conductors stood at the back door and collected fares as passengers boarded the car.

Pay As You Enter cars were soon equipped with larger, Cleveland fare boxes which were mounted near the door. Because of their appearance, they were known as "coffee grinders."

During the First World War, competition from the jitneys cut into company profits and in 1918 the fare rose to six cents. The BC Electric cushioned the blow by keeping the five-cent fare for returned soldiers, and dropping its policy of charging double after midnight.

The next increase came in 1929. Fares went up to seven cents, and stayed there all through the depression and the Second World War. Then, in 1947, in the wake of a strike by its employees, the company raised the price to ten cents.

In 1955, when the last streetcars disappeared from Vancouver streets, riders were paying 13 cents.

But the biggest change came on the first day of 1922. Canadians, true to their British heritage, had driven on the left side of the road ever since the appearance of the automobile. Naturally this confused the motoring tourists from the United States who were driving to Canada in increasing numbers. The government made the change to right-hand drive in the interior during 1921, but on the coast it delayed until the first day of the New Year, giving the street railway time to prepare for the changeover.

It was a massive job for the BCER, supervised by master mechanic George Dickie. Work began six months ahead of time. Each streetcar had a new door and steps cut into its right-hand side, then covered over in readiness. On the night of December 31, every available employee set to work unveiling the new doors, panelling over the old ones, changing track switches, modifying the signals and the stops and taking care of myriad other details. Early the morning of January 1, the first car ventured out into a changed world where everyone drove on the right side of the road. The conversion came off without a hitch, and during the first weeks of the new regime streetcars ran without a single accident.

During a trip to Eastern Canada to pur-

The first streetcar to operate on the right-hand side of the road in Vancouver pauses after completing its first run early the morning of January 1, 1922. Motorman J.C. Stewart and conductor W.J. Foster are backed onto the wye at Hastings and Boundary Road. The changeover cost half a million dollars, and brought Vancouver into line with the rest of the province which had converted the previous year.

One of the "Kangaroos," the small four-wheel Birneys in Victoria. This one is heading south toward the Outer Wharf at Government and Fort streets not long before streetcar service ended in the capital.

chase new streetcars, company officials decided that the red and cream colours of Toronto's streetcars were more attractive than the familiar BC Electric green. Vancouver cars were soon sporting the new colours, along with route number boxes prominently displayed on the roof. Two-car trains made their appearance on busy routes, and modern steel cars supplemented the older wooden vehicles. Doors took the place of the old wire gates, and heaters kept the passengers warm.

Eastern Canada gave more than a new colour scheme to the BC system. During the 1920s, ownership of the company passed increasingly out of the hands of British investors and into the hands of Canadian shareholders. In May, 1928, a new group of owners, led by Herbert Holt, the president of the Royal Bank of Canada, and A. J. Nesbitt, president of Nesbitt Thompson and Company, took control of the BCER. They formed a new holding company, the BC Power Corporation, but BC Electric Railway retained its name.

The interior of Vancouver streetcar 81. Built by the BCER in 1906, this car retained its wooden floor, wood slatted seats and clerestory roof until it was scrapped in 1950.

Teddy Lyons

Dick Gardiner

THE OBSERVATION CARS

The most popular streetcar of all was not even part of the regular system. It was the "rubberneck wagon," the open-air observation car.

There were two observation cars, 123 and 124. Built in 1909 on a design borrowed from Montreal, they remained in service for the next 41 years. The cars toured Vancouver, stopping at corners where gangs of children sang and danced for the sightseers, and were showered with pennies and nickels for their efforts.

But the best entertainment was provided by the conductors. Teddy Lyons was a born stand-up comic. His one-liners became so popular that the company publish-ed them as a book. "See that seagull?" he quipped. "It's the richest one in Vancouver. I came by here yesterday and saw her make a deposit on a new Pack-ard." It was corny, and the passengers loved it. On the other car, Dick Gardiner, a musician and magician when he wasn't a street-car conductor, kept his riders amused with a string of magic tricks.

At a pre-arranged spot along the tour, the car stopped and the conductor directed the attention of the passengers to the fancy brick-work on the building they were passing. Hidden behind a curtain on the second floor was photographer Harry Bullen. At the right moment he snapped a picture of the car and all its riders. As the car continued on its way, Bullen developed the negative and made up several prints. Taking the pho-tographs, Bullen's assistant hopped on a bicycle and set off to rendezvous with the observation car. Pedalling alongside, he dropped the picturesinto a special box where they would mysterious-ly appear for the conductor to find at the end of the tour, and to sell to the tourists for a dollar each. Bullen printed thousands of these souvenirs, which wound up in photo albums around the world.

The observation cars ran until 1950. On September 17, their last day, hundreds of people lined the route to wave farewell to a Van-couver institution.

On the first day of 1929, Vancouver merged with its neighbouring municipalities, South Vancouver and Point Grey. At a stroke, the city more than doubled in area. Passenger traffic on the streetcars increased steadily. This trend continued during the early years of the depression, as more and more people could no longer afford the luxury of an automobile. However, in time even the cost of a streetcar ticket became a luxury and like everyone else, the BCER had to tighten its belt.

As the depression drew to a close, the BCER, like many street railway companies, faced a new crisis. The system was over 40 years old, and so were many of the streetcars. Commuters appreciated the comfort and convenience of their own car. Rickety old streetcars did not offer an attractive alternative.

During the 1930s, executives from many North American street railway companies put their heads together and came up with a new vehicle which they hoped would rival the automobile. Known as the President's Conference Committee car, the PCC was lighter, smoother, faster and roomier than the old-fashioned streetcar. Several manufacturers began to produce the new PCCs, and many companies, the BCER included, placed orders. The first one, Car 400, made its Vancouver debut on January 23, 1939.

The PCCs arrived too late for New Westminster. Faced with a growing population and streetcar routes hampered by the city's steep terrain, New Westminster converted completely to motor buses by 1938, leaving the interurban lines as the only rail transit still entering the Royal City. In Vancouver, on the other hand, the future looked good for streetcars as the BCER celebrated the fiftieth anniversary of transit in February 1940.

A PCC car at Hastings and Cambie in Vancouver. The ''bow tie'' painted on the front indicates that the car has only one operator. The PCCs were a new generation of streetcars, smoother riding, faster, more comfortable. They were expected to breathe new life into electric-powered transit in the 1940s.

During World War Two, the BCER hired its first women. In June 1943 six ''guides,'' young women in navy blue uniforms, began work selling tickets and handing out information downtown. Then, in October, 11 ''conductorettes'' began working on the streetcars. Above, a motorman and his conductorette pose at the door of Car 152.

Streetcars at Main and Hastings in Vancouver in September, 1953. By this time the conversion to buses and trolley coaches was almost complete; the cars in this photograph are some of the last in the city.

A map of streetcar lines in Victoria, ca. 1940.

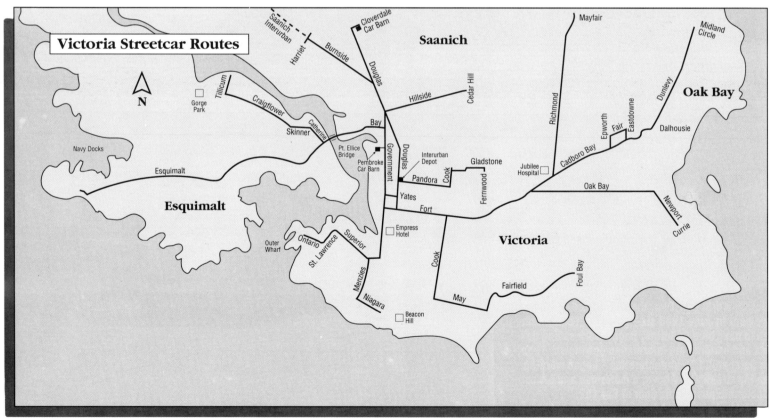

PCC Car 400 has just rolled out of the Kitsilano paint shop sporting the most radical colour change yet, the post-war BCER all-cream look. The new colours looked fine on cars, trucks and buses, but many thought it never really suited the PCCs. Also new is the company logo, a red thunderbird.

Overshadowing these celebrations, however, was the tragedy of the Second World War. Canadian Car and Foundry, the only company manufacturing the PCCs in Canada, switched to war production, and delivery of the vehicles stalled. Only 36 of them arrived in Vancouver during the course of the war, and none ever ran in Victoria.

One thing the war did bring was passengers, by the thousands. With gas and rubber tires under strict rationing, and new wartime industries running around the clock, passenger counts on the streetcars doubled, then doubled again. Every available car was pressed into service. The program underway to upgrade the fleet was dropped; even routine maintenance was neglected.

As crewmen and mechanics went off to war, the company solved the ''manpower'' shortage by hiring women for the first time, both as ''conductorettes'' and in the car barns. The BCER was one of the first companies to pay women the same as men for the same work.

When the war ended, the BCER faced the need for a thorough modernization of its fleet of transit vehicles. As a first step, the company introduced a new, all-cream colour

June 1946. A row of new, 36-passenger Brill gas buses parades past the Empress Hotel in Victoria.

The new, post-war BCER logo (above) was dubbed the "tomato bird," or even more derisively, "the worm in the apple." Tired of all the ribbing, the company soon changed the design to a large totem pole.

scheme, and a new company symbol, a red thunderbird atop the letters BCE. It also made plans to introduce more PCC cars. But first the decision had to be made whether it was wise to renew the aging streetcar fleet, along with all the track and electrical equipment. It was a tremendous investment, for a population turning again to their own automobiles. Instead the company decided to launch a ten-year program to convert the entire transit system "from rails to rubber," from the streetcars to rubber-tired buses.

In Victoria, conversion of the system actually began in 1944 when the first streetcar line was handed over to the buses. The program began in earnest in 1947 as one after another the different lines closed. Cars were offered for sale, the little Birneys going for $100 each. On July 3, 1948, crowds of people came out to ride the last cars on the last two lines, Beacon Hill and Outer Wharf. When service ended that day so did 58 years of streetcar operation in the capital.

Two days later the BCER bid official farewell to the Victoria street railway. Hung with black crepe, and with senior operator Walter Peddle at the controls, Car 383 carried a group of company and civic officials on a tour of the remaining track, around the Legislature and past the Empress Hotel for the last time. Then it was out to the scrap heap in a remote section of the CPR yards in Esquimalt.

Conversion included North Vancouver as well. The original Lonsdale line was the first to change over, in September 1946. The other two lines lasted until the following April. On April 27, 1947, members of a local railroad club chartered Car 157, decorated it with flags, and made the final run down Grand Boulevard. After their parts were salvaged, several of the cars ended up as motel cabins in the Fraser Valley. Track and trolley wire were removed, streets repaved, and within a few months all evidence of the old streetcars was gone.

It is July 5, 1948, and Car 383 passes in front of the Empress Hotel on the last trip of Victoria's last streetcar. The car is hung with black crepe and carries a group of dignitaries out to bid official farewell to streetcars in the capital.

THE LAST TRIP OF VICTORIA'S LAST STREET CAR

One of the red and cream Vancouver street-cars crosses the inter-section of Carrall and Hastings on a busy af-ternoon in the 1940s. Car 149, of the #4-Grandview Line, is pass-ing in front of the BC Electric Company's head office and depot for the interurban trams. A block away down Hastings is a Vancouver landmark, the Wood-ward's store.

A map of streetcar routes in Vancouver, ca. 1941.

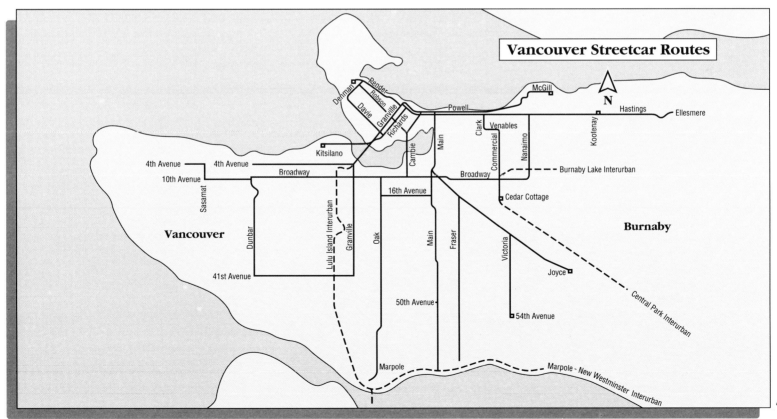

That left Vancouver, where the fleet of PCCs, steel cars and turn-of-the-century wooden trolleys attracted streetcar lovers from across the continent and beyond. But not for long. Conversion to buses began in 1947, and one by one the routes changed over. In May, 1951, the Dunbar and West Broadway lines closed and there were no more streetcars left on the city's west side.

When the streetcar systems closed down, most of the cars were burned or tossed onto the scrap heap. A few were converted to other purposes, like this unique motel cabin in Ruskin, about 65 kilometres east of Vancouver. The Ruskin Auto Camp bought several old streetcars from North Vancouver.

In 1890, when the Vancouver street railway went into operation, the original track ran down Granville Street. About 65 years later, the streetcars are gone and workers tear up the pavement outside the Hudson's Bay Store at Granville and Georgia to remove the track.

The following spring it was the turn of the Oak Street line; the old ''Toonerville Trolley'' bid farewell with a huge ceremony. When the Main Street line closed, the last of the old two-man cars with conductors went to the scrap heap, leaving just a handful of steel cars and the PCCs.

The end finally came on April 24, 1955. A special issue of *The Buzzer* invited the public out to the PNE grounds where the remaining cars were officially retired with pomp and ceremony. When Car 415 rolled into the Carrall Street depot at 6:21 p.m. that evening it was the last streetcar to give service in Vancouver.

Most of the cars were broken up for scrap and burned. The company tried to sell the PCCs but there were no buyers and eventually they too went to the scrap heap. One survivor was Car 53, an original BCER-built four wheeler that had been converted to a salt car for winter use. Employees restored it, and it went on display at the PNE. Now it sits inside a restaurant in Vancouver's Gastown.

A few others survived. One ended up as a diner in Penticton, until it was scrapped a few years later. The provincial museum has one of the Victoria Birneys, found abandoned in the bush near Cowichan Lake. And after spending all those years trundling up and down the hills of North Vancouver, Car 153 ended its days as a chicken coop on a farm in the Fraser Valley, where it was discovered and restored by the North Vancouver Museum.

A steam engine tows a long line of retired streetcars through the CPR's Drake Street yards towards the Kitsilano shops and the cutter's torch. Most of the cars were burned or broken up for scrap.

CHAPTER TWO

INTERURBANS

At the beginning of 1891, New Westminster was proudly displaying all the signs of a modern city. Electric lights were illuminating the downtown streets. A telephone service was in place. Tracks were being laid for the new streetcar system. But none of these projects was as audacious as the plan hatched by two local businessmen, Henry V. Edmonds and his brother-in-law, John A. Webster. Directors of the street railway, these two promoters decided not to stop with simple streetcars. In addition, they wanted to connect the Royal City to Vancouver by an electric rail line.

The idea seemed preposterous. Some 20 kilometres of uninhabited bush lay between the two cities. No one had built an electric railway that long anywhere in North America. But Edmonds and Webster were undeterred. They owned a sizeable portion of the land through which the line would pass and hoped to spark a profitable real estate boom. Together with Vancouver mayor David Oppenheimer, and other local businessmen, they incorporated the Westminster and Vancouver Tramway Company, later merging the street railway with it.

◄

About 1912, crewmen stand in front of one of the interurban cars about to leave the north end of the Kitsilano trestle for Steveston, via Eburne, later Marpole. The interurbans were the original form of rapid transit, carrying passengers and freight between outlying areas and the larger cities. By the outbreak of World War One the BCER operated four interurban lines on the Lower Mainland and one on the Saanich Peninsula. Note the oval tin ''wing sign,'' used as a destination sign on the early trams.

Henry V. Edmonds, a real estate developer, former mayor of New Westminster, and one of the richest businessmen in the province. He was one of the founding directors of the Westminster and Vancouver Tramway Company.

At the time, travellers from New Westminster reached Vancouver by stagecoach over the Douglas Road to Maxie's Hotel at New Brighton, then a summer resort on Burrard Inlet near the present PNE grounds. From there, the journey continued by boat down the inlet. Or they took the CPR train to Port Coquitlam where they transferred to the main line for the ride into Vancouver. A tramway promised faster, more convenient service. It would open the area to settlement, and it would connect to the new Great Northern Railway which was building south from the Fraser River across from New Westminster to Blaine, Washington.

Construction began on the combined car barn and powerhouse, a massive steam generating plant located at what is now Kingsway and Griffiths Avenue. Meanwhile, work gangs cleared a right-of-way through the dense forest, cutting down every tree that threatened to topple onto the tramway. On September 29, 1891, the first car made a trial run along the Westminster section of the line. Loaded with company officials and civic dignitaries, the car left the terminus at 8th Street and Columbia, opposite the CPR station, and went east to Leopold Place. Going up Leopold, it turned west onto Royal Avenue and continued around Clinton Place, up Park Row and along First Street past Queen's Park. Turning west again, the car made its way across to Sixth Street, where it trundled north to Edmonds Street and along to the powerhouse at the edge of settlement. Champagne was served all around, and everyone toasted the good fortune of the company.

Soon the rest of the line was complete. It continued past the powerhouse another 14 kilometres, entering Vancouver via Commercial Drive, Venables, Campbell and

The first interurban tram to New Westminster prepares to leave downtown Vancouver on October 8, 1891. The two men at the rear of the car on the left are Theodore Davie, left, BC attorney general, and Aulay Morrison, a Burnaby solicitor. The man standing in the doorway is Fred R. Glover, New Westminster city clerk and later a senior official of the BCER.

Hastings streets to the terminus at Carrall and Hastings. There were three stations along the way. One was at Glen and Venables in Vancouver, called Largen's Corner after a blacksmith who had a shop there. The second, where the line crossed the New Westminster wagon road, was called Central Park, a reference to the New York birth-

place of David Oppenheimer's wife. The third was the powerhouse itself.

In the city of New Westminster, three Patterson and Corbin, four-wheel streetcars provided local service. The company ordered four large, double-truck cars from streetcar builder J.G. Brill for the interurban line. Painted a beautiful olive green and cream,

The comparative sizes of the streetcars and trams can be seen in this 1892 photo of First Street, New Westminster. On the right, a decorated interurban car is in-bound for New Westminster. Next to it is one of the city's three streetcars, following another tramcar. In the distance, another streetcar has just turned off 3rd Avenue.

The track crew, or road gang, aboard a work car on the interurban line in 1893. The distinguished looking man with the flowing white beard standing in front is Roderick Sample, the crew's foreman.

these 10.5-metre trams, with their upholstered seats and closed-in platforms, offered the latest in luxury travel. Since the streetcars already numbered 1, 2 and 3, the larger cars took numbers 10 to 13.

Opening day for the entire line came on October 8, 1891. Without regard for superstition, Car 13 received the honour of making the first complete trip, downtown to downtown. North America's first true interurban line was now in operation.

Initially, two trains a day left New Westminster for Vancouver, one at 8:30 a.m. and the other at 4:30 p.m. Despite fares of 50 cents, or 75 cents return, which were high for the time, loads of 100 or more passengers were not uncommon. The company ordered three new cars to handle the traffic and soon offered a train each way every two hours.

The following summer, 1892, the company opened a new line, known as the 12th Street Cutoff. It carried the trams from Edmonds straight down 12th Street to Columbia, avoiding the circuitous route around Queen's Park and reducing the running time between the two cities to 45 minutes. (The cutoff was dangerously steep, and after a freight train overturned on it, killing a conductor, it was replaced in 1912 by a more gradual descent down the Highland Park Cutoff a bit farther west.)

At first, the optimism of the tramway promoters was rewarded. Settlers began opening lots along the line, and on October 8, 1892, a meeting at the powerhouse elected a reeve and councillors and incorporated the municipality of Burnaby. But the next year British Columbia plunged into the recession. Development along the tramway fell off, passenger

The interior of an interurban car, with wicker seats, brass luggage racks and a high, clerestory roof. Behind the door at the rear was a small compartment for smokers.

numbers declined, and even the freight business was not enough to save the company.

The mortal blow fell when one of the huge dynamos in the powerhouse burned out. The cost of repairs forced the company into bankruptcy. In April, 1895, the Bank of British Columbia foreclosed, and when the company's assets went up for auction Francis S. Barnard and his Consolidated Railway and Light Company bought them.

After the Point Ellice Bridge disaster in Victoria, Barnard and his partners reorganized their street railway holdings and in April 1897 the BC Electric Railway Company emerged as the owner of all the province's public transit systems, including the interurban. The new company was optimistic about the tramway's future. Work began on an extension of the line to Sapperton and two large new tram cars were ordered from the Ottawa Car Company in Ontario. After fire destroyed most of the buildings in the centre of New Westminster in September 1898, the BCER built a handsome new station and freight sheds on Columbia at Begbie.

The recession lifted, and business began to expand. The BCER turned its attention to the growing farming community on Lulu Island, a fertile delta at the mouth of the Fraser River. Fishermen from the small settlement at Steveston, and farmers hauling their produce, could only reach Vancouver over a long, tortuous road. It took an entire day to ride the stagecoach from Steveston to the city.

The CPR first realized the potential of this

On November 4, 1911, a locomotive hauling four loaded boxcars and a flatcar lost its brakes and came careening down the 12th Street cutoff in New Westminster. The train flew off the track and the locomotive turned over, pinning the conductor, Fred Cooper, and killing him instantly. Above, a crowd gathers around the wreck.

Streetcar 2 of the original Westminster Street Railway Company displays a windshield with a difference. This one-piece glass with a wood frame had a canvas bottom. It was folded down in good weather, as seen here, or pulled up when the weather was poor to give the operators some protection from the elements. Many motormen must have complained that the closed-in vestibules on the interurban cars offered much more comfort.

51

area. In July 1902, it inaugurated twice-daily service from Vancouver to Steveston via the tiny logging community of Eburne aboard the "Sockeye Limited." The BCER leased and electrified this line and on July 4, 1905, began interurban service with three new tramcars, appropriately named the "Richmond," the "Steveston" and the "Eburne," built by Thomas Driscoll in the New Westminster shops.

Expansion of the interurban network continued. In 1909 the BCER opened a further extension from Eburne along the north bank of the Fraser River to New Westminster. Eburne, which the company renamed Marpole after CPR superintendent Richard Marpole, became an important junction point.

Initially, the Steveston line terminated at

the original CPR station at the north end of the Kitsilano trestle which crossed False Creek. When the new Granville Street Bridge opened in 1909, a large station was to the Westminster and Vancouver Tramway Company, at the west end of Columbia Street and used it as a temporary depot for the interurban.

◄

George Kidd, an English accountant who came out to BC as comptroller for the BCER in 1911. He replaced R.H. Sperling as general manager of the company in 1913. Ten years later his title changed to president, a position he held until the end of 1928.

built at the south end of the bridge on pilings level with the deck. From the new station the interurban line swung west, then south along what is now West Boulevard to Marpole. The major station en route was Kerrisdale, named for Kerry's Dale, the ancestral Irish home of the wife of company manager R.H. Sperling. At Marpole, trams either turned east to New Westminster, or crossed the Fraser River to Lulu Island on a long trestle. Following Garden City Road, the line travelled south, then west beside Granville Avenue to Richmond's main station, Brighouse. Carrying on to Railway Avenue, it turned south again for the run into Steveston.

THE LAKEVIEW ACCIDENT

Early on the morning of December 10, 1909, a BCER freight train was switching cars at a pipe factory on the Central Park Line just east of Nanaimo Road. A flatcar loaded with heavy timbers was left on the main line. The locomotive coupled up to the flatcar and had just begun hauling it eastward toward New Westminster when, with a loud bang, the coupling broke. The flatcar began rolling back down the long grade toward Vancouver, picking up speed as it went.

Meanwhile, the first eastbound passenger tram, the Sumas, with motorman George Thorburn at the controls, set off from Vancouver. At a few minutes after 6 a.m., as the tram neared Lakeview Station heading up the long grade, the flatcar careened around a slight bend and slammed into it head on. The heavy timbers flew off the flatcar and kept going. They virtually sheared off the top half of the tram, killing 17 of the 23 people on board, including the crew. It was the worst transit accident in Vancouver history. The photograph above shows the Sumas shortly after it was built in 1907.

The interurban pulls in to a crowded Brighouse station, the main station in Richmond, in 1909.

A BCER electric locomotive, followed by a baggage car loaded with milk cans and three interurban trams lined up at the north end of the Kitsilano trestle. A small city streetcar brings up the rear. The locomotive was known as an "octagon" because of the strange shape of its cab.

The new interurban depot built on the southeast corner of Columbia and Begbie in New Westminster after the 1898 fire. The building was likely designed by architect W.T. Dalton. It also served as the first New Westminster office of the Great Northern Railway. Trams looped around the block to load and unload freight and passengers.

The interurban station at the south end of the Granville Street Bridge opened in May, 1914. It was thought by many to be the most handsome train station in the country. Trams from this station travelled through Kerrisdale, Marpole and Richmond to Steveston. It closed at the end of 1923 after the change in the ''rule of the road'' made loading and unloading inconvenient. A new interurban station then opened at Davie and Seymour.

The wooden trestle which carried the interurban across the Fraser River from Marpole into Richmond.

Early trams were made of varnished wood, with graceful rounded ends, or vestibules, and large wooden pilots, or ''cowcatchers.'' Each car was named for a local city or municipality. By 1910, however, a growing system required multi-car trains. Pilots and curved ends gave way to couplers and ''train'' doors so that the cars could be coupled together. The names disappeared as well, replaced by a simple number.

With their interurban lines prospering, the directors of the BCER embarked on the most ambitious undertaking of them all, a new line east from New Westminster to tap the fertile Fraser Valley.

Rich with farmlands and dairies, the Valley was the breadbasket of the Lower Mainland. But farmers had a difficult time getting their produce to market. Roads were poor; steamboats on the Fraser were slow, and could not run when the river froze. BCER officials reasoned that an interurban line to Chilliwack would bring an economic boom

to farming communities throughout the Valley, open the area to more settlement, and provide good revenues for the company, both in transportation and electric power sales.

In 1906 a group of promoters had incorporated another railway company, the Vancouver, Fraser Valley and Southern, and won a land grant for a right-of-way through Burnaby out into the Valley. No track was ever laid, however; the railway existed only on paper. The BCER bought this company to obtain the land grant and began laying track east from New Westminster.

Construction proceeded in three sections. The first section, from New Westminster across the Fraser to Cloverdale, was easier than the others, and by July 1, 1910, the

The "Surrey," one of the first interurban cars turned out by the BCER shops in New Westminster, posed with the crew that built it in 1903. Ornate trim and elaborate arched windows highlight the car. Names for the cars were later dropped in favour of simple numbers; the "Surrey" became Car 1204.

A work crew laying track through the Fraser Valley for the interurban line to Chilliwack. Work went on through the scorching summer of 1909 and many of the men came down with dysentery, which luckily was cured by generous portions of fresh milk from the local farms.

59

Before construction of the Fraser Valley Line was complete all the way to Chilliwack, service began on the section between Langley and New Westminster. On May 4, 1910, the company inaugurated its famous milk run, carrying milk cans and produce on an early-morning freight train to Vancouver. Then, on July 1, a passenger car was added to the freight car (right) and commuters rode for the first time.

A track crew blasting its way through the rocky bluffs at the foot of Vedder Mountain.

first trains were in operation between Langley and New Westminster. East of Langley, work crews had more difficulty. Right-of-way had to be cleared through dense forest, rock was blasted and bored around the shores of Sumas Lake, and load after load of gravel was dumped into the swampy low ground to provide a solid bottom. Poles erected beside the track one day sank and toppled across the rails the next.

Finally, on October 3, 1910, Premier Richard McBride boarded a specially decorated train of three new interurban cars and rode out to Chilliwack to drive the last spike. Much to the embarrassment of the BCER, the train did not quite make it all the way. A pole fell across the track near Vedder Mountain, cutting off power, and a steam locomotive had to be dispatched to tow the first electric train into Chilliwack, several hours late. Nevertheless, the city welcomed the interurban with brass bands blaring and steam whistles shrieking. "Monday the 3rd of October will rank as the greatest day in the history of Chilliwack," the local newspaper declared, "marking as it does the commencement of rail communication with the outside world..."

The Fraser Valley Line was an instant

success. Within years, all the riverboats disappeared, replaced by the fast, reliable service of the electric trams. For a $3 return fare, passengers rode the 102-kilometre line on any one of the three daily trains. Cars built for the Fraser Valley service were much larger than cars on the other lines and came equipped with restrooms. Along with passengers, they hauled farm produce, milk from the dairies, and mail for the towns along the line.

The BCER now enjoyed its greatest period of expansion. During 1911 the company built a new head office in downtown Vancouver, with a large interurban depot on the main floor. The original offices and depot in New Westminster also had outgrown themselves, and were replaced with a new facility at the corner of 8th Street and Columbia. Both buildings still stand today. The original

tramway was known as the Central Park Line, or District One. The Lulu Island Line became District Two, and the Fraser Valley Line District Three.

On June 12, 1911, the Royal City depot became the terminus of yet another route, District Four, the Burnaby Lake Line. At this time two distinct townsites were developing in Burnaby: North Burnaby, with east Hastings Street as its commercial district, and South Burnaby, centred on Kingsway. Along with the municipal council, the BCER saw an opportunity to encourage development in the central area. Like the Central Park Line, the new Burnaby Lake Line emerged from Vancouver along Commercial Drive. But at Commercial and 6th Avenue it branched off to the east, crossing central Burnaby on much the same route that the Trans-Canada Highway follows today.

At last the big day arrived, and the first train bound for Chilliwack rolled out of New Westminster. All went well until just past Vedder Mountain where a power pole had collapsed across the track, downing the power line. Much to the chagrin of BCER officials, a steam locomotive had to be called out to take the train in tow, and the first electric interurban to arrive in Chilliwack did not do so under its own power.

An interurban train circles the loop at Chilliwack Station in August, 1949. The lead car, 1304, now belongs to a museum in Glenwood, Oregon.

The pre-war boom continued. Short branch lines to Fraser Mills and Sapperton were opened. By 1912 the BCER operated a fleet of 647 vehicles on 373 kilometres of streetcar and interurban track and carried 65,581,267 passengers. Highlights of the era were the lacrosse games at New Westminster's Queens Park and the horse races at Minoru Park in Richmond, both served by the BCER. Fans flocked to these events in such numbers that the trams sometimes could not handle them and streetcars had to be pressed into service on the interurban track. When this still failed to carry all the traffic, the company borrowed passenger coaches from the CPR, or hastily arranged rows of seats on flatcars.

But not every company project turned a profit. In 1913 the BCER built a 38-kilometre interurban line up the Saanich

Above, coaches borrowed from the CPR are pressed into service on the Steveston interurban line to handle the crowds of people heading for the races at Minoru Park. These wooden coaches were the original dome cars. Left, flatcars are crowded with sports fans going to a lacrosse game in New Westminster.

◄
The BCER opened its new Vancouver head office and depot at the corner of Carrall and Hastings in 1912. Used by the company until 1958, it is now a bank.

Peninsula, north of Victoria. Like the Fraser Valley, the peninsula was a breadbasket of dairies and fertile farms, ripe for settlement and expansion. The new line ran from downtown Victoria up the centre of the peninsula to Deep Bay, with a short spur over to Patricia Bay. Premier McBride again drove the last spike on June 18, riding out on a decorated train of three new St. Louis cars, the latest style of tram purchased from the St. Louis Car Company.

The new line started out well enough, but freight and passenger traffic soon fell off. Distances were not as great as in the Fraser Valley. Many farmers found it easier to load

At the Deep Bay terminus, an operator poses beside Car 23 on the Saanich Peninsula interurban line. Originally a Victoria streetcar, Car 23 was converted to interurban use, than back again when the Saanich line closed. It is 1924, the last year of the line's operation.

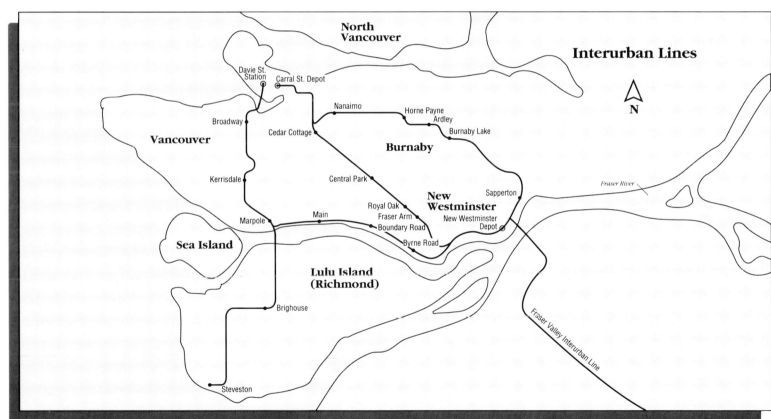

A map of the interurban lines on the Lower Mainland.

◄
An interurban train waits at Marpole Station in May, 1951.

Right, a milk train on the Fraser Valley line heads for New Westminster through the rural countryside near Meridian. Every station had a milk platform, which early every morning was crowded with shiny silver milk cans waiting to be loaded on the train. Outbound from New Westminster in the evening, the milk train brought the cans back filled with water for farms without wells. Eventually the line had a fleet of ten baggage cars used almost exclusively for the milk business.

By the end of the 1930s, it was cheaper to ship milk and other produce in trucks. The milk train made its final run on February 18, 1939.

For small loads of freight on the Stave Falls line, the BCER used this GMC truck outfitted with railway wheels to make the 10-kilometre run from the Falls to Ruskin.

their produce onto wagons and truck it straight into Victoria rather than to transship with the railway. There were several good roads up the peninsula, a reliable bus and jitney service, and even a rival railway, the Victoria and Sydney.

In 1919 the Victoria and Sydney closed, but the fortunes of the interurban did not improve. Declining freight and passenger revenue finally forced total abandonment of the line in 1924. Today, only street names such as Interurban Avenue mark the route of the big trams.

Elsewhere, however, business was good. Special milk trains raced in daily from the Fraser Valley. More and more commuters rode the streetcars and trams. The BCER began to consider other projects: an extension of the interurban from Chilliwack to Rosedale, a bridge connecting Steveston and Ladner, a new line from New Westminster to Ladner. But before any of these plans could be implemented, World War One intervened.

The war absorbed many of the company's young employees and much of its resources, eliminating the possibility of expansion. Freight tonnage showed an increase, but passenger traffic fell off, especially when the jitneys spread into the suburbs.

The end of the war unleashed a new mood of expansion in the company. In 1921 it took over the Western Power Company of Canada and its development at Stave Falls, 65 kilometres east of Vancouver. As part of the takeover, the BCER acquired a short railway running north from the CPR line at Ruskin to the Stave Falls power dam. Once electrified, this small interurban, miles from the main system, supplied the Stave dam and another dam built at Ruskin a few years later.

A passenger waits for the interurban at the Tod Inlet shelter, about half way up the line, near today's entrance to Butchart Gardens. Passenger traffic never did become great enough to make the Saanich train a success.

A map of the Fraser Valley Line, from New Westminster to Chilliwack.

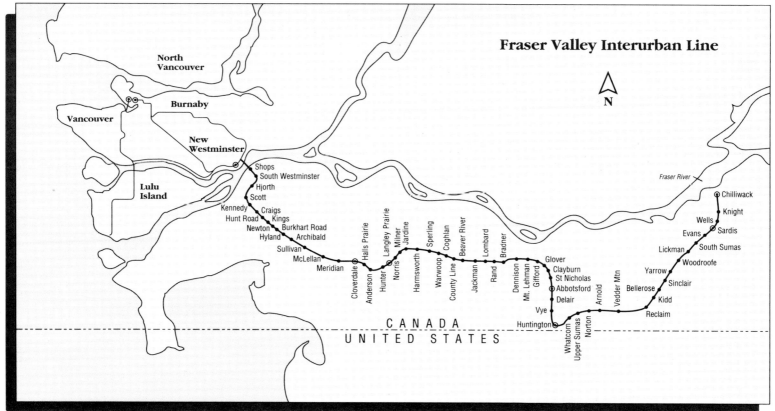

Fraser Valley Interurban Line

N

North Vancouver

Burnaby

Vancouver

New Westminster

Lulu Island

Fraser River

Chilliwack

Shops
South Westminster
Hjorth
Scott
Kennedy
Hunt Road
Craigs
Kings
Newton
Burkhart Road
Hyland
Archibald
Sullivan
McLellan
Meridian
Cloverdale
Anderson
Halls Prairie
Hunter
Norris
Langley Prairie
Milner
Jardine
Harmsworth
Sperling
Warwoop
Coghlan
County Line
Beaver River
Jackman
Lombard
Rand
Bradner
Dennison
Mt. Lehman
Gifford
Glover
Clayburn
St Nicholas
Abbotsford
Delair
Vye
Huntington
Whatcom
Upper Sumas
Norton
Arnold
Vedder Mtn
Reclaim
Kidd
Bellerose
Sinclair
Yarrow
Woodroofe
Lickman
South Sumas
Evans
Sardis
Wells
Knight
Chilliwack

CANADA
UNITED STATES

During a severe winter storm in January 1916, the streetcars closed down and parts of Victoria were cut off from food and fuel. When rail service once again got moving, the army was called out to distribute coal and other supplies to people in their homes. In thanks for their help, the BCER allowed soldiers to ride free on the Victoria streetcars for two months.

A Shay steam locomotive belonging to the Western Canada Power Company on the Stave Falls line prior to the BCER takeover.

Below, the Gifford station, near Abbotsford, floats away during the 1948 flooding in the Fraser Valley. It took almost three weeks to restore full service on the interurban line.

By the 1920s the population of the Fraser Valley was almost four times what it had been in 1910. Passenger counts were well up. The old dark green trams were repainted red with cream trim. New stations sprang up to handle the increased use of the system.

The interurbans gave reliable service, but every once in a while the weather conspired to close the system. In January 1935, Vancouver recorded its worst snowfall ever. Freezing rain, snow and sub-zero temperatures caused huge snow drifts and coated the power lines with thick ice that brought them down. The Fraser Valley was hardest hit; no trains ran for several days. As crews restored power and cleared snow, the line reopened bit by bit and the BCER used buses to keep service going.

Flooding was just as serious as the occasional snowstorm. The spring of 1946 brought heavy floods in the Valley, washing out parts of the interurban line. Once again,

► A stream of interurbans and city streetcars pass up and down Hastings Street on a busy afternoon in 1931. The photograph, looking east, was taken from an upper floor of the BCER head office at Hastings and Carrall. The interurban depot was on the main floor.

buses provided emergency service. But by far
the worst flooding occurred in May, 1948,
when a heavy spring runoff burst dams and
dykes throughout the Valley. Water over
three metres deep covered all the low land
from east of Chilliwack right through to

New Westminster and Richmond. Stations
floated away; great lengths of track were
washed out. It was mid-June before the
water receded and full train service was
restored.

The BCER tightened its belt during the
depression years of the 1930s. Layoffs
were held to a minimum, though the system
as a whole ran at a loss, and service on some
lines was reduced. In 1937 the company replaced its New Westminster streetcars with
buses, and at the same time closed the interurban service to the Fraser Mills east of
town. The Burnaby Lake Line was cut back
to Sapperton, where trams met a connecting
bus service to the New Westminster depot.
In the Fraser Valley, the last of the milk
trains ran on February 18, 1939.

But these changes did not herald an end to the interurbans. The outbreak of World War Two inaugurated the busiest period of ridership that the company ever experienced. Gas was rationed, and workers rode the streetcars and trams to the growing war industries around Vancouver. The army established a large base and training camp at Chilliwack, and troop trains travelling back and forth from the city became a familiar sight in the Valley.

"Reddy Kilowatt," the cartoon character, became the new company symbol of cheerful efficiency. But not all employees were as content as their cartoon colleague. On January 9, 1945, motormen, conductors, bus operators and maintenance crews walked out on strike. The interurbans to Steveston and Chilliwack remained in service because their crews belonged to a different union. All the same, on January 11, pickets stopped the trams from leaving their barn in Kitsilano. The government did not tolerate a wartime transportation strike for long. The regional labour board stepped in, awarding employees a raise of four and a half cents per hour and a

better pension plan. Work resumed on January 19.

Business boomed after the war and the BCER looked forward to improving freight revenues. At the same time, the increased use of private automobiles was cutting into passenger counts. Faced with an aging fleet of trams, the competition of the automobile, and suburban settlement that was spreading away from the interurban lines, company directors turned to a cheaper, more flexible mode of transport, the motor bus.

On the Fraser Valley Line, its very design was now its undoing. Originally, tracks were laid to meander through every small community. In the post-war period, automobiles using new roads could drive through the Valley much faster than the interurban. A formal application was made to abandon all passenger service to Chilliwack.

On September 30, 1950, two trains decorated with bunting and flags set off from opposite ends of the line. Crowded with dignitaries from the valley communities, and officials of the BCER, the trains met at Langley

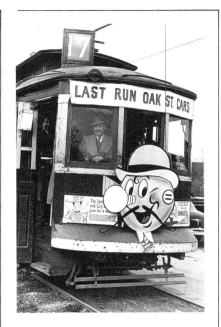

With an electrical socket for an ear, and a light-bulb for a nose, Reddy Kilowatt was adopted as a marketing symbol by privately-owned hydro-electric utilities all over the world. Reddy was a familiar face to transit riders in BC where the BCER used him in all its advertising. When the provincial government nationalized the transit company in 1961, Reddy, a symbol of private enterprise, disappeared.

A 21-passenger White bus at Broadway and Commercial in 1932. The owner of the fish and chip shop stands next to the bus. At this time the BCER used buses principally as feeders for the interurbans and streetcars.

During the flooding in the Fraser Valley, passengers and freight were transferred from the interurbans to buses to complete their trip. Because they were not confined to a track, buses proved more convenient than the trams.

for a short ceremony and luncheon. Guest of honour was 71-year-old Bert Johnson, motorman on the first tram out of New Westminster 40 years earlier. Trains on the Fraser Valley Line carried only freight from that day on.

Streetcars were disappearing from city streets as well, replaced for the most part by new buses and trolley coaches. One route the trolleys began serving in Vancouver was Arbutus, running along the interurban line to Marpole. With bus service in place, there was no longer any need for the interurban,

and on July 17, 1952, the last tram was retired from this section of the line.

Next to go was the Burnaby Lake route. The central areas of Burnaby never did develop the way the BCER hoped and the line was not a money-maker. Passenger service was hourly; freight was almost nonexistent. Finally, on October 23, 1953, the line was abandoned completely. Tracks were lifted, and today almost no trace of them remains.

Less than a year later, on July 16, 1954, it was the turn of the Central Park Line.

When the last train, loaded with retirees, rail fans and well-wishers, reached New Westminster it ended 63 years of service on North America's first interurban line. Three decades passed before history came full circle and the old line once again came alive with the opening of Vancouver's new SkyTrain.

The New Westminster depot was now a lonely spot, served only by the interurban to Marpole. When that line, too, closed, on November 18, 1956, the depot was sold to Wosk's and became an appliance and furniture outlet. Today it is a Value Village store.

That left the line between Marpole and Steveston. Everywhere else the streetcars and interurbans were gone; shiny new buses and trolley coaches ruled the roads. The final curtain rang down on February 28, 1958.

Two special trains, decorated with ribbon and bunting and carrying Reddy Kilowatt on their fronts, made the official last trip. Among the civic and company officials and special guests on board was George Boston, the motorman with the longest record of service on the line. He had started with the CPR on Lulu Island, then transferred to the BC Electric when it took over in 1905. Known as the ''Candy Man,'' he always had a pocketful of sweets for the kids who rode his tram, the ''Red Rocket.''

When the moment came, motormen Barney Kady and Joe Metcalf applied power for the last time, moving their trains slowly out of the old Marpole station heading for Steveston, 12.6 kilometres away. With them went the last moments of the BC Electric interurban service.

Dal Grauer, president of BC Electric. Raised on a farm on Sea Island, he was a Rhodes scholar who left university life to join the BCER as general secretary in 1939. He became president following the war.

As crew members look on, BCER President Dal Grauer, left, shakes hands with Langley Reeve G. Brooks as their two trains from opposite ends of the Fraser Valley line meet in Langley. The ceremony, on September 30, 1950, brings an end to interurban service to Chilliwack.

CHAPTER THREE

BUSES AND TROLLEYS

PART ONE:
MOTOR BUSES

In the new-found prosperity of the ''Roaring Twenties,'' Vancouver and its suburbs grew rapidly. The streetcars and interurbans of the BC Electric formed the backbone of the transportation system, but recently a new vehicle had crowded its way onto city streets: the ''horseless carriage,'' the automobile.

The automobile first made its presence felt just before the First World War. In 1918 there were 10,000 of them registered in British Columbia; by 1923 the number had swelled to 47,000. Starting during the war, the infamous jitneys were organized into bus and taxi companies to compete with the BCER. Legislation gave the BC Electric exclusive rights to pick up passengers in the city, and protection from the jitneys. But the bus was a more serious rival.

◄
In 1909, this early bus ran from the Harrison Hotel at Harrison Hot Springs to pick up guests at the CPR station in Agassiz. The first buses were actually just large automobiles, sometimes ''stretched'' to handle more passengers. It was the 1920s before vehicles built as buses began to appear on regular routes.

The BCER itself first considered using buses, and trolley coaches, as early as 1912 to serve some of the sparsely populated areas of the city. But these early vehicles had unreliable motors, solid tires, and poor, if any, suspension. It was not practical to run them on unpaved and gravel roads.

By 1923 the situation had changed. The new Grandview area was developing on Vancouver's east side quite a distance from public transit. Streetcars went east on Broadway only as far as Nanaimo, and south on Commercial Drive to 15th Avenue. Broadway and Commercial was a major focal point for transit on the east side, just as it is today with the advent of SkyTrain. To reach the new housing areas, the BCER thought about extending streetcar service along Broadway east to Renfrew, then south to 22nd Avenue. The estimated cost of the new route was $329,000, very high for the time. This included an expensive and somewhat hazard-ous ''diamond'' crossing on Renfrew just south of Broadway where the streetcar line would intersect the tracks of the Great Northern and CNR railways. A less costly solution was to try a bus.

The BCER asked the White Motor Company, one of the largest and most reliable bus and truck manufacturers, to supply a 14-foot wheelbase frame, or chassis, with a 30-horsepower engine. On this frame the company placed a 21-passenger bus body built by G. W. Ribchester, a Vancouver firm.

The route led east on Broadway from the streetcar transfer point at Broadway and Commercial to Grandview Highway, out the highway to 13th Avenue where it turned east again to Renfrew, then south on Renfrew to 21st. There it jogged over to Slocan to clear the creek, then carried on east along 22nd Avenue to Rupert. Proposed service was a bus every 30 minutes.

On March 16, 1923, the BCER took delivery of the new bus. Painted the company's standard colours of dark green with the name BC Electric in gold, it was an impressive sight for many of the veteran streetcar men at the Prior Street car barn where the vehicle would be housed. It sported the number M1, the letter denoting a motorbus, just as L stood for linecar and S for sweeper.

The next morning general manager George Kidd hosted a trial run over the new route. Along with Kidd for the ride were Vancouver mayor Charles Tisdall, J. Horne-Payne, son of the company chairman, and several other dignitaries. The driver was R.L. Dickie, later the company's first bus supervisor.

Regular service began Monday, March 23, from 6 a.m. to midnight. It was an instant success. Within a month, the company ordered a second White bus, the M2, to offer 15-minute service in the peak periods. The route was later lengthened, along with the buses which were rebuilt to carry 29 passengers.

The BCER was now fully into the bus business. When the University of British Columbia moved to its new location in Point Grey in 1925, the company purchased six

Below, BC Electric's first bus out for its inaugural run in 1923, loaded with dignitaries. Left, the interior of an early bus looking toward the front door.

Above, the first motor buses purchased by the BCER as they looked after their bodies were stretched. The tank in the background is the BCER coal gas storage tower in the company's Carrall Street yards. Right, one of the Leyland buses which began running out to UBC in 1925. The body was wooden, and the engine was cranked by hand to start.

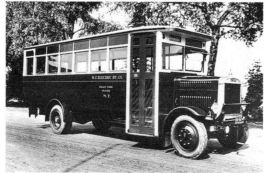

Leyland buses to operate out 10th Avenue to the new campus from a bus garage at 10th and Trimble Street. At the same time, intercity buses began running along Kingsway to New Westminster, out to the Fraser Valley and south to White Rock and beyond.

The first buses had few of the conveniences modern drivers take for granted. A row of lighted candles across the base of the windshield took the place of a defroster, at least until the glass shattered! Theoretically, vehicles were heated by a bypass from the exhaust pipe. But gas fumes leaked so badly that it was seldom used. Cold wind howled up through the holes cut in the floorboards to accommodate the gas, clutch and brake pedals. Drivers bundled up in layers of coats, sweaters, gloves and scarfs, and loathed to unbundle to sell tickets or make change.

In the thick fogs so common in Vancouver then, the job of navigating was not an easy one. Off-duty drivers came in to act as fog pilots, standing in the doorway to warn their partner away from the curb, or trotting on ahead trailing a white handkerchief.

The first bus in Victoria, a Yellow Coach on the Haultain line in 1929.

The BCER also began a bus service in Victoria in December 1929 with the opening of the Haultain line, still a bus route today. Three handsome new Yellow Coaches, the forerunner of General Motors, offered a 15-minute service from downtown. But the BCER was not the first in the field. Not only did Victoria have the honour of starting the first street railway in the province, it inaugurated bus service as well, in the form of a small horse-drawn omnibus company in business long before 1890. Then, in the jitney era, another company, Veterans Transportation, began operating the Blue Line.

At 10th Avenue and Sasamat, students bound for UBC transfer from a streetcar to one of the new buses under the watchful eye of a BCER inspector.

The forerunner of to-day's articulated buses, a 1936 Ford Tri-Coach bus poses at the corner of Pender and Beattie in downtown Vancouver. This strange-looking vehicle was nicknamed "The Snake" because of the way its front end swivelled around corners. It was one-of-a-kind and ran until the late 1930s.

Many early bus companies grew out of jitney operations that flourished during the First World War. In Victoria, one of the leading bus companies to compete with the BCER was Veterans Transportation, operators of the Blue Line. In 1948, BC Electric took over Blue Line and ran it as a sightseeing business called Royal Blue Line. Right, the company's ticket office.

Another of the jitney operations was the Flying Line, which in 1923 carried riders between Victoria and Sydney in this Packard touring car.

Headed by the Sangster family, pioneer jitney operators, Blue Line offered regular service to Oak Bay and Haultain in competition with the BC Electric buses and streetcars. By 1929 Blue Line was running 19 buses, and had branched into sightseeing as well.

As if competition was not fierce enough between the BCER and Blue Line, a third company entered the field. Vancouver Island Coach Lines (VICL), the large intercity bus company that ran the length of Vancouver Island, took over some of the old jitney routes. Under manager John Matson, VICL began the Burnside, Gordon Head and Lakehill routes north of Victoria, leaving Blue Line and BCER to compete in the west.

The three-way battle for passengers continued until 1948, when BCER took over Blue Line, partially keeping the name for its sightseeing business, Royal Blue Line. The remaining two companies agreed that BC

Electric would run city service, and Coach Lines would stick to the intercity routes.

In many ways it was the competition from buses in Victoria that forced the BCER to remain as flexible as it could, contributing to the early demise of streetcars in the capital and the decision not to introduce trolley coaches.

Meanwhile, the Vancouver bus fleet was growing. In 1930 the summer-only Spanish Banks line began service. Buses met bathers at the 4th and Alma streetcar terminus and carried them out to the beach. During the depression, *The Vancouver Sun* newspaper chartered additional buses to bring children to the beach for free. Within a few years, Spanish Banks service became year-round.

Top left, a Mack bus in the Blue Line fleet. Bottom, a Blue Line Hayes bus, now in BC Electric hands. Note the new name, Royal Blue Line, and the BCE symbol.

During the 1930s The Vancouver Sun newspaper offered free swim classes for the kids in Stanley Park. The BCER drove the young swimmers to the park for free aboard this 1925 Leyland bus. The driver, Don Leatherdale, poses with a few of the youngsters.

July, 1934. The swimming pool bus is now a White model vehicle. The tents belong to The Vancouver Sun's free swim school.

During the Thirties, a few more bus routes were added, mainly to supplement the streetcar lines. Then, August 3, 1936, saw the first true replacement of a streetcar line by a bus. The new Cambie-King Edward route came up Cambie Street from Broadway to King Edward, then west to Granville, ending the King Edward streetcars.

In New Westminster, buses made an immediate impact. With houses spreading away from the streetcar lines, the BCER decided to convert the Royal City completely to the new vehicles. The first bus rumbled through the streets of the city in 1936. By the next summer the conversion was almost complete. On July 20, following a ceremony and

Two brand new Mack buses, the first with the modern flat front and rear engine, parked at the New Westminster shops in 1937. The first motor bus appeared in the Royal City in 1936, and by the following summer, every streetcar line except one had closed.

Left, one of the buses which arrived in Vancouver wearing its wartime "uniform." This one is a 1942 Twin Coach, unique for its rear engine.

"bus banquet" at Queens Park, Mayor Fred Hume cut a ribbon on Columbia Street and bus service began on all lines. The streetcars were gone completely the following year.

By the eve of the Second World War the Vancouver bus fleet numbered 25 vehicles, and was about to enter its busiest period. Transit was used so heavily during the war that the government's war allocations board in Ottawa became responsible for new bus orders for all Canadian cities. The board was headed by Sig Sigmundson, who later became transportation manager for the BCER. Buses began arriving in Vancouver painted their wartime colours of olive green or grey, and were quickly placed in service.

With the end of the war, and the "Rails to Rubber" program well underway, bus service really expanded. New Fageol, Ford and Brill vehicles arrived from the factory in the new cream paint scheme with the red BCER thunderbird emblem. Service began in Richmond to augment the Lulu Island interurban, in South Burnaby on the Smith-Rumble lines to supplement the Central Park interurban, and in north Burnaby where the BCER took over Neville Stage Lines, a large private company that connected with the streetcars.

These three bus models joined the Vancouver fleet following the Second World War. Top, a 34-passenger, Fageol Twin Coach; centre, a Ford Transit; and bottom, two Brill gas buses. The Brill on the right shows the original "worm in the apple" insignia, while the one on the left shows the later, thunderbird variation.

For years streetcars in North Vancouver had crossed McKay Creek on a high, wooden trestle. In 1943 the trestle was condemned, forcing the BCER to shorten its Capilano line. The company began a shuttle bus service to cover some of the streetcar's former route. Left, passengers transfer from the bus to the streetcar at Fell and Marine.

In North Vancouver the BCER introduced its first buses during the war. Operating out of a garage next to the old car barn at 3rd Street and St. David's, the buses replaced the last of the streetcars on the North Shore in 1947. The following year it was the same story in Victoria. The streetcars were gone, replaced by motor buses working from the Pembroke Street car barn and the new Garbally Road bus garage a few blocks to the north.

In Vancouver, the move was to electric trolley coaches, with motor buses running mainly on feeder routes. Knight-MacDonald was the main motor bus route; it actually was slated to take trolley coaches until engineering studies showed that the Burrard Bridge would not carry the steel poles neces-

Workers at the Cambie Garage at the end of the Second World War. In the background, Twin Coaches in their drab, wartime colours.

◄ Policemen gather information from eye witnesses following a bus accident in Vancouver.

The "Safety Bus" in 1954, used by BC Electric to carry the message of bus and road safety to the schools.

sary to hold the trolley wire. The garage at 10th and Trimble closed in 1953 and all buses were assigned out of Cambie Garage at Cambie and 16th Avenue, or Oakridge at 41st and Oak Street.

In 1958 the company brought in the first diesel-powered Brills as Richmond converted to an all-bus service with the closure of the last interurban line. And with the end of the North Vancouver ferry later that year, North Vancouver buses began running through to downtown.

The Brill diesels turned out to be the last new buses bought by the BC Electric Company. On August 1, 1961, just a few days after the death of BCER president Dal Grauer, Premier W.A.C. Bennett ended months of speculation and rumour by announcing that his government was taking over the BC Electric as part of its plans for hydroelectric power development in the province. The next year the government created a new Crown corporation, the BC Hydro and Power Authority, and the name

Driver Ernie Tuscon appears to be wondering what to do with this passenger. This photograph was used to advertise the circus at the 1958 PNE.

One of the small Brill gas buses in Victoria sporting the new BC Hydro logo and colours in the 1960s.

BC Electric disappeared.

The changeover became visually apparent when buses began sporting the new BC Hydro colour scheme, white with blue and green striping and the Hydro symbol. New buses arrived for Victoria, in 1963, and North Vancouver, in 1964, the first of the General Motors "new look," or "fishbowl" diesels, one of the most popular designs ever built.

One of the most sweeping changes in transit occurred on April 1, 1970, when Hydro introduced the "exact fare" program and bus drivers no longer carried change. Fares had climbed from six cents on the original bus in 1923 to 25 cents, with tickets long since replaced by tokens. With exact fare, the tokens disappeared as well.

Above, one of the new GM "fishbowl" diesels, with green and blue BC Hydro stripes, in operation in North Vancouver. Left, another North Vancouver motor bus of an older vintage, a Twin Coach, stopped on Capilano Road. The operator, near the front door, is Bill Clark.

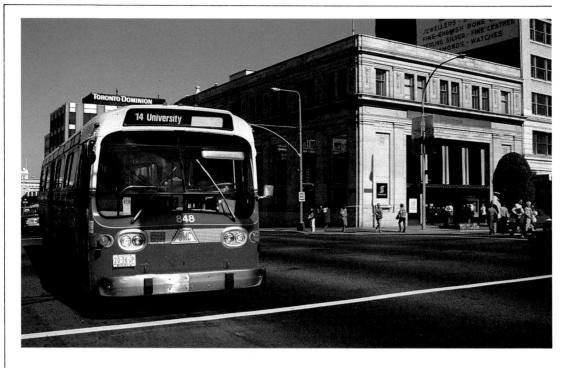

Vancouver was growing, and growing even faster were the municipalities surrounding it. Transit ridership was in a slump during the 1950s and 1960s with so many people preferring to use their own cars. By the mid-1970s, however, the energy crisis and increased traffic congestion caused commuters once again to turn to public transit. The government was quick to respond. It set up a new Bureau of Transit Services within the ministry of municipal affairs to direct the funding and planning of transit. Bus service extended into the suburbs, taking over from private bus operators, or from the earlier intercity service operated by Pacific Stage Lines. A much larger part of the Lower Mainland was now receiving full transit service. BC Hydro still operated the vehicles, but this period saw the beginning of a process of separating transit from the hydroelectric utility.

In 1978, a new Crown corporation, the Urban Transit Authority, took over the responsibilities of the Bureau of Transit Services. BC Hydro continued to operate transit in Vancouver and Victoria until 1980 when a

► A modern Flyer diesel bus in Vancouver in the BC Transit colours adopted in 1984.

new operator, the Metro Transit Operating Company, took over. At the same time, local governments began to play a role in funding and planning transit in their communities. BC Hydro was now out of the transit business.

In August 1982, the Urban Transit Authority became BC Transit, a name more reflective of the corporation's province-wide responsibilities. Vehicles adopted a new red, white and blue colour scheme. The Metro Transit Operating Company continued in existence for three more years until, with plans underway for the new SkyTrain rapid transit service and expansion to bus routes on both the mainland and Victoria, Metro Transit merged with BC Transit in 1985. Since that time a single authority, BC Transit, has had responsibility for public transit everywhere in the province.

PART TWO:
TROLLEY COACHES

One of the first of the larger, T-48 Brill trolleys to arrive in Vancouver in 1949.

One morning in early December, 1945, a BC Electric line crew arrived at the corner of Pender and Burrard in downtown Vancouver and began stringing trolley wire west towards Georgia Street. There was nothing unusual about this, except that in place of the usual single strand of streetcar wire the men were stringing two wires, 600 millimetres apart. They were for the latest type of transit vehicle on Vancouver streets, the electric trolley coach.

The trolley coach was developed in Germany in 1882, but it did not see much use in Canadian cities until the late 1930s. Faced with competition from the private automobile, many street railway companies considered replacing their old streetcars with the modern PCC car, or the motor bus. But transit companies owned and operated by electric utilities, such as the BCER, found the trolley coach a more attractive alternative because it utilized the cheaper source of power and the overhead wires and feeder systems that already existed.

Trolley coaches made in Great Britain or the United States were operating successfully in Edmonton, Winnipeg and Montreal, but at the end of the Second World War there were no Canadian manufacturers. Since the BCER was happy with its fleet of motor buses built by the Fageol Twin Coach company,

A line crew stringing
trolley wire in Vancouver
ca. 1948.

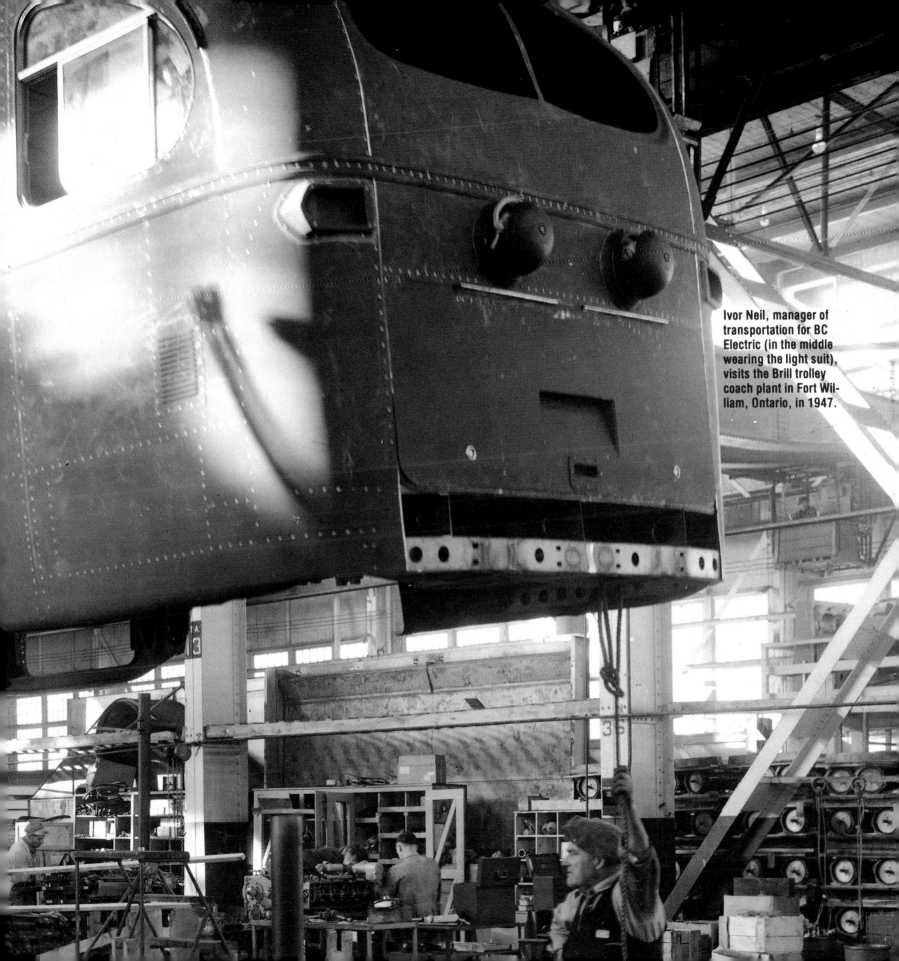

Ivor Neil, manager of transportation for BC Electric (in the middle wearing the light suit), visits the Brill trolley coach plant in Fort William, Ontario, in 1947.

Right, the first electric trolley coach in Vancouver passes in front of the Marine Building on a test run, December 5, 1945. The bus was on loan from Seattle, one of the earliest major cities in North America to switch from streetcars to "trackless trolleys." The coach arrived by railway flatcar, and after preliminary trials in Victoria, came over to Vancouver.

Sunday, August 15, 1948. The day before regular service begins on the new Vancouver trolleys, the company offers free rides to all comers. Passengers wait to board one of the coaches at 29th and Cambie. By 1955 new trolley coaches would replace every streetcar in the city.

it made arrangements to borrow a Fageol trolley coach from nearby Seattle and to operate it as a demonstrator in both Vancouver and Victoria in December, 1945.

The test runs met with great success. The riding public appreciated the smooth, quiet, comfortable ride, and liked the convenience of a vehicle that, unlike the streetcar, pulled right into the curb to pick up passengers. In Victoria other factors outweighed the success of the trials, chiefly the competition from two other motor-bus companies. The BCER decided to replace streetcars in the capital with new motor buses, and the borrowed test vehicle retains the distinction of being the only trolley coach ever to run on the island. In Vancouver, on the other hand, the trolley coach was the obvious choice. Over the subsequent decade it formed the backbone of the "Rails to Rubber" conversion program.

The Fageol company, pleased with the success of the borrowed Seattle coach, hoped to obtain a large order from BC Electric. But in the aftermath of the war, Canadian Car and Foundry, builder of BC Electric's PCC cars, announced that it was offering its parent company's Brill trolley coach. The BCER quickly signed up to buy the new vehicle.

The manufacturer rushed two coaches through production for delivery in July 1947, in time to be displayed at the annual Pacific National Exhibition. Numbered 2001 and 2002, they introduced Vancouver to a new form of electric transit that is still going strong today, and to the new, post-war company image. Gone was the old red and cream of the streetcar era. An all-cream colour scheme took its place, with the letters BCE on a red background topped by a symbol of the West Coast, the Indian totem pole.

The two trolleys were the first of an original order of 30 coaches. But even before the BC Electric completed plans for the first route, it ordered 12 more vehicles, then a further 40. The company also acquired a former army barracks at 41st Avenue and

Ivor Neil, BCER's general manager of transportation, poses with officials of CCF-Brill in front of the company's first trolley coach demonstrator, painted the manufacturer's colours of green and cream. The BCER bought 30 of the buses to inaugurate trolley service in Vancouver. Left, inspecting the controls of the new trolley.

Trolley 2001 in the Kitsilano shops being prepared for display at the PNE in 1947.

Above, Little Mountain Garage, the temporary bus depot at 41st and Cambie, formerly an army barracks and parade square. Gas buses of every size and description are lined up for service. At the rear of the yard, rows of new Brill trolley coaches await their first day on the job. On the same weekend in August, 1948, that trolley service was inaugurated, the BCER opened its huge, new Oakridge Transit Centre, right. Today, of course, the forest that surrounds the Centre in the photograph has been replaced by housing.

Cambie Street to use as a temporary bus depot while work began on the $1,750,000 Oakridge Transit Centre on 14 acres of land a few blocks away at 41st and Oak Street.

Inauguration of the city's first trolley coach route was set for Friday, August 13, 1948, on the Fraser-Cambie line. An impressive guest list of politicians and trade and industry officials was on hand, hosted by BC Electric President Dal Grauer, Vice-President E.W. Arnott and transportation manager Ivor Neil. After a ceremonial

ribbon-cutting opened the new Oakridge Centre, guests toured the buildings, then boarded the trolleys for a ride. At 7th and Main Street, President Grauer asked the driver of his coach, Harold McLean, for a turn at the wheel. McLean obliged, and with a smile Grauer proceeded to pull out into traffic, dewire and break a trolley pole.

On Sunday, August 15, all the trolleys went into service, giving free rides to the public. And ride they did, mobbing every coach on the line. Early the next morning regular service began when operator Charlie Street drove the first of the new vehicles out the gate.

The first trolley coaches were 44-passenger models, the T-44s. In 1949 Canadian Car and Foundry offered a larger, 48-passenger model with double-wide front doors. This quickly became the standard BC Electric model, and the company did not purchase any more of the smaller coaches.

The first three T-48s, costing $24,500 each, arrived at the Kitsilano shops in May 1949. As conversion proceeded on one streetcar route after another, more and more trolleys arrived to take up their new duties. On January 28, 1954, the final order of coaches arrived from Canadian Car's factory in Fort William, Ontario. BC Electric now boasted Canada's largest trolley coach fleet, 327 Brills.

The conversion of the last streetcar line along Hastings Street on April 24, 1955, ushered in a new era of bus and trolley coach service in British Columbia. The special "Rails to Rubber" edition of *The Buzzer* marking the event reviewed the history of the streetcars but ended with a picture of a trolley coach crossing the new, eight-lane Granville Street Bridge, symbolizing "the most modern metropolitan transit system in the nation."

An aerial view of Granville Street at Dunsmuir in 1951. Streetcars are still running on Granville, but not for much longer.

Friday, August 13, 1948, three days before regular trolley service will begin in Vancouver, officials go for a ride. Eight trolleys are lined up on Pender Street between Beatty and Cambie, ready to roll into operation. The original route began at Marine Drive and Fraser. The trolleys followed Fraser north to Kingsway, jogged across to Main Street and continued down Main to Pender. Turning left, they went as far as Seymour before turning south to Robson Street, then left to Cambie and south as far as the terminus at 29th Avenue.

Five trolley coaches side-by-side on Hastings Street near Renfrew during the Pacific National Exhibition in August, 1955. Hastings is the only street in North America where this scene is possible, because it is the only street with five sets of overhead trolley wires. The coach in the centre of this photograph, 2040, has been restored to its original BCE colours.

Unhappily, it was also the beginning of a recession that peaked in the late 1950s. Housing starts fell off, and business and consumer spending declined, especially in the automotive industry. Manufacturers of fancier cars, such as Packard and Studebaker, folded, while cheaper, smaller European imports, like the Volkswagen Beetle, became more popular. When Ford tried to turn things around with a new luxury car, the Edsel, it failed miserably.

However, with less money being spent on automobiles, one thing the recession did bring was an increase in transit ridership, and a need for more trolleys. Sig Sigmundson was transit manager for the BCER. Noting that several Canadian cities were building up their trolley fleets with used coaches from the United States, he decided to do likewise and arranged to buy 25 Pullman-Standard vehicles from Birmingham, Alabama.

The Pullmans arrived by railway flatcar at the Kitsilano shops early in 1957. The company was surprised at the weight of the new coaches. Made of steel, they were almost twice as heavy as the aluminum Brills. Since few Canadians ventured into the American South, mechanics were also surprised at the notices inside the vehicles announcing segregated seating for "Negroes."

The company spent a lot of money redoing the Alabama coaches for Vancouver service and the first one went into operation on March 7, 1957. Operators found them awkward to drive and they were assigned mainly to the 41st Avenue and Broadway lines which were flat and straight. But the increase in ridership was not as great as Sigmundson anticipated and within three years the Pullmans were pulled from service and sold for scrap. Vancouver once again became an all-Brill city.

During the 1960s, BC Hydro, the Crown

corporation that had taken over transit, made a moderate extension to trolley coach service. But it also announced plans to phase out trolley service altogether and to replace it with modern, more flexible diesel buses. As in so many other places across North America, the electric trolley coach appeared to be on the way out in Vancouver.

However, the one thing the transit industry did not count on was the global fuel crisis of the 1970s. Oil was in short supply; prices skyrocketed; lineups formed at service sta-

tions; air pollution and the environment were suddenly of concern to everyone. The handful of cities still running electric transit, including Vancouver, gave up any idea of exchanging their clean, pollution-free vehicles for diesel burners.

By this time, no manufacturer was making new electric trolleys. Toronto modernized its fleet by rebuilding the controls of its old Brills, then buying new bodies from Flyer Industries in Winnipeg. Edmonton did likewise.

#2416, the last of the Brill trolley coaches. When these vehicles finally retired, each had logged over 1.6 million kilometres of service. This particular bus was preserved and has been restored to its BC Hydro colours.

Right, two trolley coaches pass on the Granville Street Mall in the heart of Vancouver's commercial and entertainment district. Opened in 1974, the mall is a stretch of Granville given over to pedestrians and transit vehicles only.

Since 1980, the needs of disabled passengers have received special attention from transit planners. One result is that in Vancouver, new diesel buses have automated lifts for disabled riders. Right, Debbie Krentz, a manager for Pacific Transit Cooperative, tries out one of the new lifts, along with Helen Cook, a custom transit planner with BC Transit.

BC Hydro was next to order 25 of the new Flyer vehicles. The first two arrived in December 1975, with the balance of the order arriving during the following spring. Meanwhile, the last of the original 44-passenger Brills were phased out.

From the original fleet of trolleys, that left the T-48s. They were still operating, but they were getting old and maintenance was increasingly difficult. Finally, the decision was made. Vancouver would continue with clean, quiet, pollution-free electric transit. BC Transit, which now had responsibility for transit vehicles, placed an order with Flyer for 245 new trolley coaches with state-of-the-art electronic controls.

▶
A modern Flyer trolley coach on Granville Street in downtown Vancouver. The coach displays the red, white and blue colour scheme adopted in 1984.

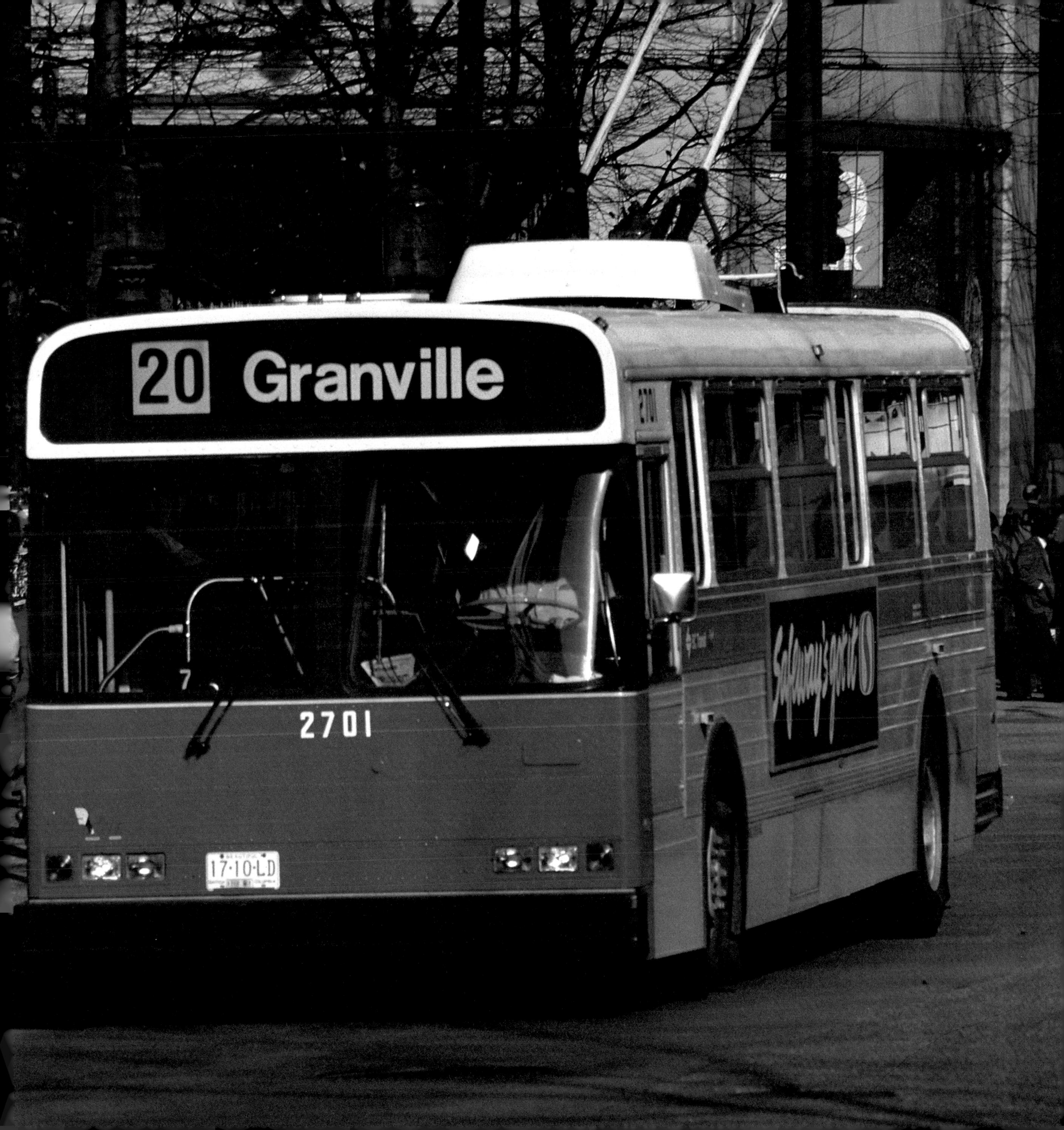
20 Granville
2701
17·10·LD

During the 1970s the original Brill trolleys were phased out, replaced by new-look Flyers like the one above, pictured with BC Hydro officials on its inaugural run, Dec. 31, 1975.

The arrival of the new generation of trolleys, with their smart styling, large destination signs and chopper controls, spelled the end for the remaining Brills and one by one they came out of service. By January 1984, only a handful remained. Plans were made for a brief, final run and, much to the surprise of the organizers of the event, hundreds of transit fans showed up on the special day, January 14, to ride a Brill for the last time. It was a fitting tribute to a vehicle that served the city so faithfully for so many years.

But the Brills still had the last laugh. Vancouver suffered through a harsh winter that year and when salt on the city streets got into the modern electronics of the new Flyers, sparks began to fly. The new trolleys began breaking down. While mechanics tried to find "non-saline" solutions to the problem, the remaining Brills were pressed back into service and kept running for several more months. Eventually, though, the problem was solved and the Brills were gone for good.

BC Transit is still committed to the energy-efficient, clean-running trolley coach. Elsewhere on the continent the trolley, like the streetcar before it, has almost passed into history. But Vancouver has added major extensions to its trolley lines. In 1986 trolleys began running from the Joyce Loop terminus out to the Metrotown shopping centre and SkyTrain station in Burnaby, the first time a trolley line extended beyond the Vancouver city limits. And in September 1988, trolleys began running out to the University of British Columbia campus along a route that was converted from diesel buses back to trolleys, quite the reverse of transit trends over the past decades.

Other cities, notably Seattle and San Francisco, have joined Vancouver in looking at extending and modernizing their trolley coach systems. For BC Transit the next step may be more route extensions and the introduction of larger, articulated trolleys. In any event, Vancouver is assured of smooth, quiet and clean electric transit for many more years to come.

One of the new Flyer trolleys arriving in Vancouver in 1982.

On the left, a Hess articulated trolley coach borrowed from Europe by BC Hydro for testing. It is parked next to a Brill at the Oakridge Transit Centre in the mid-1970s.

In 1986 trolleys began running beyond Vancouver city limits. This one connects the Joyce Loop terminus with Metrotown shopping centre and SkyTrain station in Burnaby.

FROM DIESEL TO TRIESEL

During Expo 86, the largest fair ever held in British Columbia, BC Transit mustered every bus in its fleet to carry the thousands of visitors who daily took transit to the fairgrounds. To meet the demand the corporation dragged out of storage some of the original Flyer 2600 trolleys, the ones with the re-built Brill motors. Painted the new BC Transit colours of red, white and blue, the 2600s did yeoman service for the duration of the fair.

Out of service once again, the old Flyers took on a new life. Some of the older diesel buses in the fleet were suffering body problems, though their engines and running gear remained sound. Transit employees conceived the idea of putting diesel motors in the old Flyer trolleys, converting them to ''triesels.'' Work began on converting all the remaining 2600s, and the project was completed in 1989. Above, electrician Dennis Williams works on the conversion.

One of Vancouver's 244 trolleys, the second-largest trolley fleet in North American, after San Francisco.

PART THREE:
PACIFIC STAGE LINES

Ivor Neil, founder of Pacific Stage Lines and later general manager of transportation for BC Electric.

In the early spring of 1912 a young man disembarked from a CPR train in Vancouver with only a suitcase in his hand and a few dollars in his pocket. Ivor W. Neil, a native of Wales, soon found lodging in his adopted city and a job at the Stock Exchange.

While "I.W.," as he soon became known, worked away at his stocks and bonds, the streetcars and interurbans were facing stiff competition on the streets of Vancouver. The automobile had become a way of life during the First World War, and many owners were operating jitney services. After the BCER succeeded in having their rivals banned from areas served by the street railways, many jitney owners formed taxi companies, or had their touring cars "stretched" and went into the bus business.

One of these transit entrepreneurs was Ivor Neil, who quit his job at the Stock Exchange and launched a taxi and sightseeing business during the war. Neil struck up a friendship with another ex-jitney driver, Goodman Hamre, who started one of the first bus companies in the province in 1914. In 1919 Hamre sold part of his business, the bus route between New Westminster and White Rock, to Neil.

In 1922 Neil bought some more buses, opened a new route between Vancouver, Port Moody and Coquitlam, and reorganized himself into a new company, Pacific Stages Transportation Ltd. The company soon acquired others, until Neil was running buses up the Fraser Valley to Haney and south to Seattle.

While Neil was busy expanding his operation, the BCER was also getting into the intercity bus business. Another group of jitney operators, headed by the Coldicutt family, had banded together to form the Blue Funnel Lines, operating between Vancouver and New Westminster via Kingsway. The BC Electric did not have service on Kingsway, but Blue Funnel was competing with the

An early tour bus leaving the North Vancouver ferry on its way to Capilano Canyon ca. 1915.

A PSL White bus, ca. 1928. This vehicle ran between Vancouver and Port Haney and the lady on the left was a regular passenger every day for years.

A White model bus belonging to Pacific Stage Lines, outside the Central Hotel in White Rock in 1926. This was still the era when buses were simply stretched automobiles, or bodies mounted on truck chassis. The White carried 22 passengers, and each row of seats had its own door.

Central Park Line of the interurban. Not liking the competition, the BCER bought it out, purchased six new Fageol buses, and on May 1, 1924, began operating under the name BC Rapid Transit. Service soon extended to Port Moody, Port Hammond, Port Haney, Essondale and Coquitlam.

In December, the BCER formed a subsidiary, BC Motor Transportation Ltd., under which it merged several competing companies, including Ivor Neil's Pacific Stages. The tour companies were reorganized as the Gray Line, while the intercity bus lines were consolidated under a new name, Pacific Stage Lines (PSL), with Ivor Neil in control.

As Neil supervised the expansion of his new company, he recognized the need for a new terminal. The old Pacific Stages operated out of a storefront in the Swain Building at 724 West Hastings in downtown Vancouver, using the curb as a loading platform. Early in 1926 ground was broken for a new depot and office building on the southeast corner of Dunsmuir and Seymour streets, and by autumn it was ready. It was written up in trade journals of the day as the most modern bus depot on the continent.

A Seattle-bound bus pauses on the Chuckanut Drive, south of Bellingham, Washington, in 1929. This was one of the new Yellow Coaches built specifically for the Seattle run. Luggage was carried in pontoons on the roof, and the trip took nine hours. Ivor Neil is standing next to the bus.

Gray Line was the tour bus branch of Pacific Stage Lines. Left, four Gray Line buses wait for passengers outside the Great Northern train station in Vancouver in the early 1930s.

From 1924 to 1932, BC Rapid Transit was a subsidiary of BC Electric. In addition to buses, it operated a freight line in the Fraser Valley. This truck, towing two pup trailers, is leaving the New Westminster depot.

A busy Vancouver bus depot at Dunsmuir and Seymour in 1938. When it was built in 1926, the depot was considered the most modern on the continent. The bus in the foreground is a Hayes ''Clipper.'' The other two buses are ''Teardrops.''

Three years later the new Cambie Garage opened to handle the servicing of the growing fleet of buses. PSL was now running buses through West Vancouver to Horseshoe Bay, through Surrey to Hall's Prairie, Coast Meridian and Johnston, past Haney to Mission and Harrison Hot Springs, and out to Sumas Prairie. Neil's 20-odd buses were racking up 1600 kilometres daily.

The only company the BCER did not include in its creation of BC Motor Transport was BC Rapid Transit. This operation had extended service to Chilliwack, and on June 12, 1927, made the bold move of sending buses 65 kilometres up the Fraser Canyon. On June 1, 1931, service reached Kamloops. Eight-passenger Studebakers made

The interior of the Pacific Tour and Travel Bureau office in the Vancouver bus depot in the 1930s. Posters indicate the incredible expansion of bus service throughout the province.

three trips weekly, leaving Vancouver at 7:25 a.m. and arriving in Kamloops 13 hours later.

In 1932, BC Rapid Transit finally merged with BC Motor Transport under Pacific Stage Lines. Over the next few years the last remaining independents were absorbed. The Kamloops and Seattle service later was sold to Greyhound, and PSL concentrated on its Lower Mainland and Fraser Valley routes.

The buses themselves took on a new look at this time. The stretched automobiles, or bodies with seats on a truck chassis, gave way to the true intercity buses of today. In 1936 a local manufacturer, Hayes, revolutionized the industry by coming out with a streamlined model based on the Chrysler Airflow. It was nicknamed the ''Teardrop,'' and proved so successful that Hayes became the main builder of PSL vehicles. To match the new image of modern service, the company adopted a new emblem, Pegasus, the flying horse, to signify strength, speed and beauty.

A Blue Funnell bus and driver in 1931 up the Fraser Canyon. Blue Funnell was one of the bus companies that grew out of jitney operations during the First World War. It joined the BCER family in 1924.

A popular destination for vacationers was the ivy-covered Harrison Hot Springs Hotel up the Fraser Valley at Harrison Lake. Right, one of PSL's Hayes ''Teardrop'' buses arrives at the hotel in August, 1937.

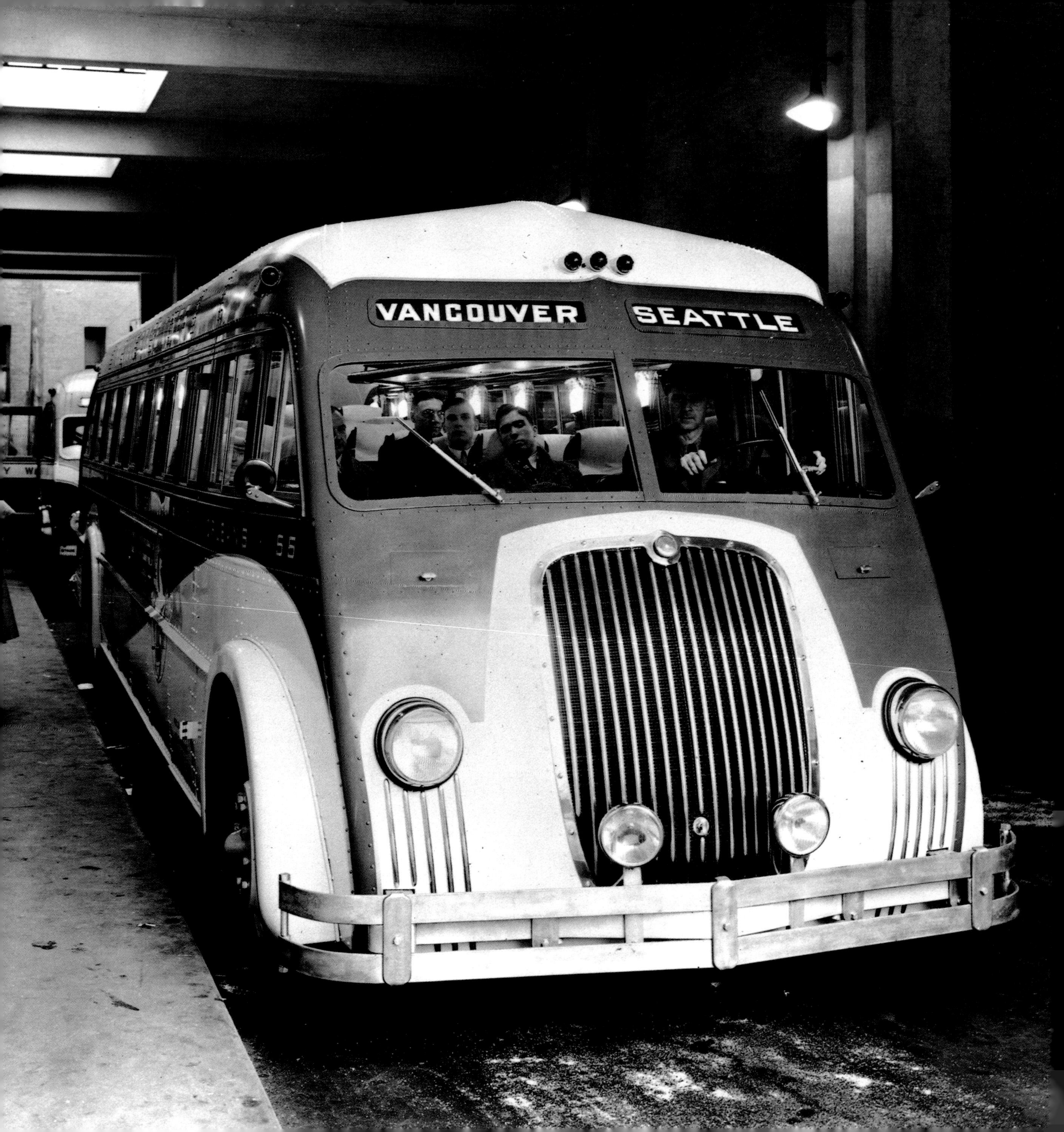
VANCOUVER
SEATTLE

Inside a Hayes "Clipper" in 1938 with passengers reclining in modern comfort. Only five "Clippers" were ever built.

◄
Opposite page, the Hayes "Teardrop" was the pride of the PSL fleet. First built in 1936, it featured distinctive, flowing lines. Here, one leaves the Vancouver depot with passengers bound for Seattle.

A PSL "Teardrop" pulls out of the Vancouver depot in 1937 bound for Horseshoe Bay. The new colours of green and cream are painted in the streamlined design of the 1930s.

A Pacific Stage Lines Courier bus boarding the ferry for Vancouver Island on the ''Royal Victorian'' service which began in 1960.

One of the Brill highway buses which were the backbone of the PSL fleet during the 1950s and 1960s, in its familiar Gray Line colour scheme.

The Second World War was hard on the province's transit systems, and by the end of the conflict it was evident to the directors of the BCER that their equipment had taken a beating. A 10-year program began to replace streetcars with new motor and trolley buses and to change the venerable old interurbans to new PSL buses. The company made arrangements with Canadian Car and Foundry to supply their new Brill intercity bus to PSL.

With the cancellation of the interurban to Chilliwack in 1950, PSL built new depots and facilities throughout the Fraser Valley.

But the biggest move of all was to a new Vancouver terminal. The beautiful building at Dunsmuir and Seymour, completed in 1926, had grown too small. PSL now had close to 300 employees, carried over five million passengers a year, and operated 16,000 kilometres of bus service daily. To meet its expanding needs, the company leased Larwill Park, a playground at Dunsmuir and Cambie, and built a new, $300,000 terminal, which opened on July 31, 1947.

During the 1950s BC Electric concentrated on building up the passenger bus business and slowly the name BC Motor Transport disappeared. In June 1960, when ferry service started between Tsawwassen and Sidney, PSL joined with Vancouver Island Coach Lines to offer through service between Victoria and Vancouver.

Pacific Stage Lines continued to operate as a subsidiary of BC Electric, and later BC Hydro, until April 1, 1979, when it merged with Vancouver Island Coach Lines to form a separate Crown corporation, Pacific Coach Lines. With the new company went the last ties to the old transit system.

Vancouver Island Coach Lines was the main operator of intercity bus service on the Island. Left, one of the company's Hayes Leyland buses departs the CN station in Vancouver for Island destinations in 1936. Below, a modern VICL coach in front of the legislature in Victoria. The company merged with PSL in 1979 to form a new Crown corporation, Pacific Coach Lines.

CHAPTER FOUR

MODERN TIMES

Public transit in British Columbia has come a long way from the little, four-wheel electric trolleys that toured the streets at the turn of the century. Yet in some ways, the ultramodern Sea-Bus and SkyTrain which represent the very latest in transit technology are throwbacks to the early days of commuter transportation.

Take SeaBus, for example. These highly manoeuvrable aluminum vessels sprint back and forth across Vancouver's harbour at speeds up to 11.5 knots. But many Vancouverites recall the old ferry that gave reliable, if leisurely, service across Burrard Inlet for many years earlier in the century. When SeaBus appeared in 1977, it was both a reincarnation and an innovation.

Likewise, SkyTrain is an old idea in modern dress. Speedy train service linking New Westminster and downtown Vancouver originated 100 years ago with the construction of the first interurban tram line through the uninhabited wilds of Burnaby. In fact, the elevated guideway that carries SkyTrain today follows most of the route first used by the interurban's Central Park Line in 1891.

◄
SkyTrain is the newest addition to the transit fleet in British Columbia. Opened in 1986, the rapid transit train connects downtown Vancouver with Surrey, and further extensions are planned.

Right, the forerunner of today's SeaBus, the ferry St. George, named after A. St. George Hamersley, a local lawyer and land developer. Between 1903 and 1907, Hamersley operated the North Vancouver ferry. The St. George was the pride of his fleet, capable of carrying almost 1000 passengers and a dozen teams of horses with wagons. Later, under municipal ownership, the St. George was rechristened the North Vancouver No. 2.

The original Second Narrows Bridge, with its centre span open to allow boat traffic through. The bridge, opened in 1925, provided the first road link across Burrard Inlet.

The needs of commuters have remained constant over the years. Only the technology has changed to meet those needs with improved service.

The original ferry service from the North Shore began in 1866, not long after Sewell Moody took over the Burrard Inlet Mills and the surrounding settlement became known as Moodyville. This irregular ferry service carried passengers across to the summer resort at New Brighton, near the present site of the PNE. Later in the century, development in North Vancouver shifted westward to the vicinity of Lonsdale Avenue, and in 1900 ferries began regular commuter service from the Lonsdale pier across the harbour to the wharf at the foot of Carrall Street.

Over the years the ferries grew large enough to accommodate horses and wagons, then several automobiles. In 1909 service began to the foot of 14th Street in West Vancouver. As car traffic increased, however, so did pressure to have a bridge crossing to the North Shore. In 1925 the Second Narrows Bridge opened. The original span was a wooden trestle bridge, with a set of railway tracks running between the two lanes of car traffic. In September, 1930, a

freighter collided with the middle section. It was the depression, the owners of the bridge could not afford to fix it, so it remained closed for the next four years.

Meanwhile, plans went ahead for a bridge to connect downtown Vancouver to the British Properties residential subdivision in West Vancouver. Completed in 1938, the Lions Gate Bridge was privately owned and operated until the province purchased it in 1955.

With two North Shore crossings in place, and commuters preferring the convenience of their own automobiles, the harbour ferry seemed unnecessary. Service to West Vancouver ceased after the war; the ferry to North Vancouver continued for another decade, then sailed into retirement in 1958.

No sooner were the ferries gone, than the public demand for some sort of ''third crossing'' to the North Shore grew insistent. Year by year traffic on the bridges increased, as did the time it took harried commuters to make their way to and from work every day.

In 1974 the province decided to ease traffic congestion by re-introducing a North Shore passenger ferry. If commuters took a ferry to work, fewer buses and private automobiles would clog the bridges.

The province wanted a ferry unlike anything in use elsewhere. The vessel had to be fast, fuel efficient, able to get into and out of terminals in the minimum amount of time, and manoeuvrable enough to dash safely across a busy harbour.

In the early 1950s, a North Vancouver bus crosses Lions Gate Bridge into Stanley Park. The bridge was completed in 1938 as a private development to connect Vancouver with the British Properties. With the completion of the bridge, the ferry service to West Vancouver seemed unnecessary, and it ended in 1947.

The ferry across Burrard Inlet returned in modern dress in 1977 with the inauguration of SeaBus, a high-speed marine passenger service. Sea-Bus now transports more than three million people a year across the harbour. Right, one of the two SeaBus ferries passes alongside Canada Place, the waterfront trade and convention centre built for Expo 86. Moments later the ferry enters the floating terminal on the Vancouver side of the harbour.

Left, an elevated walkway connects the SeaBus passenger terminal with the former Canadian Pacific Railway station at the foot of Granville Street.

The result was SeaBus, built completely in British Columbia. The two SeaBus vessels are double-ended so that no time is lost turning around after leaving the terminal. Constructed of lightweight aluminum and powered by four diesel engines, they cross the harbour in 12 minutes. Burrard Inlet is crowded with freighters, tugs, barges, seaplanes and pleasure boats. SeaBus ferries can move in any direction—including sideways—to avoid other traffic. They are able to stop in their own length, and, because they are double-ended, either end can become the stern or the bow in an instant.

The original ticket machines for SeaBus were the first ticket machines ever used in the transit system.

Each SeaBus ferry has a capacity of 400 passengers per trip. The 12-minute voyage across the harbour offers a panoramic view of Vancouver and the North Shore, and a ride on SeaBus has become a ''must'' for visitors to the city.

Right, a SeaBus ferry in one of the terminals. A ferry can unload its passengers and take on a new load in just 90 seconds.

Below, a cutaway view of the former Canadian Pacific station, showing the ramp leading down to the SeaBus terminal. Built by the CPR during the First World War, this beautiful building was refurbished as an important part of Vancouver's integrated transit system where buses, SkyTrain and SeaBus meet and exchange passengers.

In order to minimize turnaround time, the SeaBus floating terminals are equipped to handle large numbers of passengers efficiently. A specially designed flow-through loading system keeps boarding and exiting passengers completely separate. It takes a vessel just 90 seconds to disembark a full load of passengers, take on another load and set off across the harbour.

The SeaBus commuter ferry began regular service in June 1977. Today it carries more than three million people a year across the harbour. It was the first marine transit system of its kind anywhere in the world. Fully integrated with SkyTrain and bus service in Vancouver and North Vancouver, the reliable SeaBus can be counted on to deliver its passengers in weather awful enough to block the bridges and shut down the buses.

At the same time as SeaBus was in the planning stages, it was becoming increasingly clear that Vancouver needed a rapid transit system to carry it into the next century. Conventional transit services were approaching maximum capacity, and existing roads would soon be unable to handle traffic demands. After studying various alternatives, the provincial government announced in 1980 that it would fund an Advanced Light Rapid Transit (ALRT) system for Vancouver. This was SkyTrain.

The SkyTrain concept was appealing for many reasons. The ALRT system of lightweight railcars running on their own guideway avoided the congestion of the streets. SkyTrain sweeps in and out of town at its own speed, without concern for rush-hour traffic tieups. At a cruising speed of 80 kilometres an hour, SkyTrain is capable of handling up to 30,000 people an hour in the peak direction, the equivalent of a major multi-lane freeway.

Just like the tramway that preceded it, SkyTrain is powered by electricity. It produces no exhaust emissions itself, and it reduces the number of diesel buses driving into the city centre every day. As well, the train uses less energy per passenger than either a bus or a private automobile.

SkyTrain was designed by the Urban Transportation Development Corporation, a former Ontario Crown corporation. Construction began in 1982 on the first phase of the project, a 22-kilometre line between New Westminster and the Vancouver waterfront. By the following spring, a short demonstration section was ready for trial use. Target date for completion of the entire line was 1986, when Vancouver was scheduled to host a world exposition. Fittingly, the theme of Expo 86 was transportation.

The captain of the Sea-Bus controls the ferry from a glass-enclosed bridge by operating two joysticks which control the vessel's direction and speed. On the return trip, the captain simply swivels his seat to face in the opposite direction.

SkyTrain runs along an elevated guideway that keeps the trains separate from the congestion of city streets.

For most of the way to New Westminster, the SkyTrain guideway travels six to eight metres above the ground on steel-reinforced, concrete columns. Each of the concrete beams which carry the elevated guideway weighs about 100 tonnes. Beams were pre-cast, then hauled to the construction site six at a time on long, custom-built trucks. This operation took place in the pre-dawn hours when city streets were empty of traffic. Tall cranes hoisted the massive beams into position on the columns. The process was repeated, night after night for nine months, until every one of the 1044 beams was in place.

The SkyTrain guideway to New Westminster consists of over one thousand concrete beams. Right, a specially designed flatbed truck hauls one of the massive beams to the construction site. Hauling was done at night to avoid traffic. Once at the site, above, a crane lifted the beams into place.

It took nine months, and a workforce of 5000 men and women, to erect the SkyTrain guideway.

SkyTrain elevated guideway under construction near the site of Expo 86. The large ''ball'' is now the Science Centre.

SkyTrain avoided the disruption, and expense, of running a line through downtown Vancouver by using the Dunsmuir Tunnel, built in 1931 by the CPR to move cars from its yards on False Creek to the station on Burrard Inlet. Renovation of the tunnel took three years, left. Below, a cutaway of Burrard Station, one of two underground stations on the Line.

◄
There are 17 stations along the SkyTrain line. Left, Burrard Station, one of the major downtown stations, under construction. Buses now run as feeders to Sky-Train stations.

◄

A view of Main Street
Station, one of 17 sta-
tions along the SkyTrain
line.

SkyTrain was opened of-
ficially on December 11,
1985, by Premier Bill
Bennett. After a ceremo-
ny at Waterfront Station,
the Premier and other
dignitaries boarded a
train and travelled to the
New Westminster end of
the line, left, where an-
other ceremony took
place. Below, Premier
Bennett, centre, Provin-
cial Secretary Grace
McCarthy and New
Westminster Mayor Tom
Baker unveil a plaque
commemorating the
kick-off.

Thanks to a labour force of 5000 workers, SkyTrain came through on time. On December 11, 1985, in a ceremony reminiscent of the launching of the first streetcars, Premier Bill Bennett declared the system open. For eight days over the Christmas season the public rode the trains for free. Then, with the system well broken in, SkyTrain officially launched service on January 3, 1986.

When it began, SkyTrain was at the leading edge of high-speed transit technology. The 114 cars are powered by linear induction motors (LIMs), the first use of this type of motor on an intermediate rapid transit vehicle. Each car has two LIMs mounted on the undercarriage. Unlike conventional car motors, they have no moving parts and do not directly drive the wheels and axles. Instead, they are electric motors stretched flat. Reacting with a wide steel plate laid down between the rails, the motors create an electromagnetic force which pulls the vehicle forward. When the current is reversed the car brakes electromagnetically. A pair of power rails running along the side of the tracks delivers electrical power to the trains. Essentially, the wheels on a SkyTrain car are along for the ride; they do not propel the vehicle, nor do they provide primary braking power.

In normal service, a SkyTrain train consists of four cars. Each car has seating for 40 passengers, plus standing room for another 35 to 40. Here, a two-car train is seen leaving a station.

Commuters looking out the window of Sky-Train as it speeds down the track at 70 kilometres an hour think that they are riding a train with no driver. And in a sense they are correct. Each train operates automatically. Even if they are not present in the cars, however, trained operators are keeping a close watch on every SkyTrain-vehicle from their command post in South Burnaby.

The Control Centre is the "brain" of the SkyTrain system. Every train, and each of the 17 stations, are in constant visual communication with operators at the centre via closed circuit television and video display screens. Operators at the Control Centre always know exactly where every train is along the length of the system. At the same time, computers on board each vehicle "talk" to the computers at the Control Centre. Several times each second these conversations relay information about the vehicles' speed, location and the state of on-board equipment. Other computers control the speed of the trains and tell them where and when to stop. Yet a third level of computers carries out management chores: scheduling, communicating with passengers and monitoring train equipment.

THE BLUE BUSES

Ferry service to West Vancouver began on November 8, 1909. The West Vancouver Transportation Company operated a 35-passenger gas boat, the West Vancouver, bringing prospective buyers across to look at the real estate. A second vessel was added to the service, and the municipality bought both vessels in 1912 when it took over the ferry service.

At about the same time, West Vancouver launched its own bus system to connect with the ferries. In fact, West Vancouver boasts the oldest continuously operating city bus company in North America. The first bus was a large, seven-passenger touring car. Originally the ferry arrived at Ambleside, and the ''bus'' ran back and forth between the pier and Dundarave. As housing sprawled farther west, the buses followed and the fleet grew in size.

Shortly after the Lions Gate Bridge opened in 1938, West Vancouver buses began taking passengers across the bridge into downtown. Once ferry service ceased in 1947, bus service was a vital link across the inlet.

Following the Second World War, Pacific Stage Lines and the municipal buses competed for West Van riders heading into town. As part of a campaign to keep the local vehicles in business, commuters were urged to ''Ride the Blue Bus—It's Yours.'' The public responded, and the West Vancouver Blue Buses are today an integral part of the Vancouver Regional Transit System.

The BC Parkway runs for 19 kilometres beneath the SkyTrain's elevated guideway. The 50-acre linear park, developed with both corporate and government funds, includes paths for joggers, strollers and cyclists, flower gardens, and playgrounds for children.

141

A passenger boards a bus in Castlegar, one of the smaller communities which takes advantage of the partnership arrangement with BC Transit to provide local transit service. The bus is an Orion, designed and built in Canada and used widely in the smaller communities.

SeaBus and SkyTrain are highly visible examples of the adaptation of public transit to modern times. But transit has also experienced rapid expansion of services in smaller communities throughout the province. Prior to 1970, buses in these communities were operated by private companies, or in a few cases by the municipalities themselves. These services were hit hard by the decline of transit ridership in the 1950s and 1960s. By 1970, they were in financial difficulties.

Recognizing this, the provincial government offered funding for the smaller communities in 1972. With the creation of the Urban Transit Authority in 1978, this program expanded and within a few years close to 30 transit systems were in place around the province.

BC Transit, as the successor to the Urban Transit Authority, helps to fund and plan the local operators, but local governments play an important decision-making role as well. The actual operation of the buses is contracted out to private operators, with the exception of Nanaimo, Powell River and Nelson, where the municipalities operate their own bus fleets.

In 1980 the provincial government began providing custom transit for disabled people through its handyDART program. The province took over from local service groups which had been filling the need on a non-profit basis. The handyDART program—DART stands for Dial-A-Ride Transit—provides door-to-door service in special, lift-equipped vans for riders unable to use conventional transit vehicles. In Greater Vancouver, handyDART carries about half a million passengers each year.

As well as Vancouver and Greater Victoria, handyDART is also available in a dozen municipalities around the province.

In rural areas and smaller communities, the Paratransit program has been offering special transit service since 1982. Small vans, some on fixed routes, others on demand, provide a valuable service for seniors and people who have disabilities.

Meanwhile, the Vancouver Regional Transit System is steadily making its fleet of vehicles accessible to disabled riders. SeaBus and SkyTrain are fully accessible to wheelchairs already, and new buses and trolleys are being equipped with special lifts. By 1995 half the fleet will be converted.

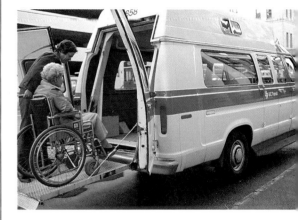

Since 1980, people who have trouble using conventional transit services have been able to get door-to-door service through the handyDART program. The handyDART vans are all equipped with wheelchair lifts.

100 YEARS OF TRANSIT
1890 · 1990
VANCOUVER · VICTORIA

British Columbia celebrates 100 years of public transit in 1990. The centennial logo, above, will be displayed on all transit vehicles as part of the celebrations. Right, SkyTrain was completed in time for the opening of Vancouver's world exposition, Expo 86. The train passed right next to the grounds of the exposition on False Creek.

Public transit in British Columbia has seen many important milestones since the inception of streetcar service in 1890: the growth and decline of the interurbans; the famous "rails to rubber" program following the Second World War; the rapid extension of transit service to communities around the province since 1972.

The 100th birthday celebration marks another milestone, this time an ambitious expansion of rapid transit service in the Lower Mainland. The second century of public transit has already begun with the extension of SkyTrain from New Westminster to Surrey. The train crosses the Fraser River on SkyBridge, a 616-metre cable-stayed bridge, the only one in the world designed solely for rapid transit use. Commuters travelling from

SkyTrain leaves Royal Oak Station in Burnaby.

SkyBridge was built to carry SkyTrain across the Fraser River from New Westminster into Surrey. Opened early in 1990, the bridge is used exclusively by rapid transit. Further extensions will carry Sky-Train to Whalley Town Centre and Coquitlam by the middle of the 1990s.

Passengers unloading at Stadium Station. More and more businesses and recreational facilities are locating within an easy walk of the Sky-Train line.

Surrey by SkyTrain can now reach downtown Vancouver in half the time it would take them using car or bus.

But the Scott Road Station in Surrey will not long remain the terminus of SkyTrain. In 1989 the provincial government revealed plans to spend another $1 billion on rapid transit in Greater Vancouver. At the head of the list of projects is an extension of Sky-Train to Whalley Town Centre. Scheduled for opening in 1993, the new line will bring Whalley within 40 minutes of downtown Vancouver.

SkyTrain will also be extended toward Coquitlam; it is expected to arrive at the

Lougheed Mall between 1993 and 1995. To the south, BC Transit is considering a rapid transit service between downtown Vancouver and Richmond, including a link to Vancouver International Airport. It has been more than 30 years since the interurban tramway through Richmond closed.

Plans also call for a third SeaBus vessel to the North Shore, a fleet of large, articulated buses and trolleys for use on major transit corridors, and a feasibility study into a rapid-transit passenger ferry between Port Moody and the downtown Vancouver Sea-Bus terminal.

One hundred years ago, public transit

played a crucial role in urban and suburban development. As streetcar tracks spread out into the virgin timber at the city's edge, settlement followed. Businesses were eager to advertise that "cars pass the door." The old electric trolleys influenced the size and shape of the city.

As the second 100 years begins, public transit once again is a catalyst for development. SkyTrain alone has attracted $5 billion worth of direct investment along its length. Large commercial, recreational and residential developments choose their locations within easy access of public transit.

But it is not the same world as it was 100 years ago. Conservation and pollution, words that the streetcar promoters did not know, are now important factors in transit planning. In its second century, public transit has the challenge not just of stimulating growth, but of helping to solve the problems associated with growth—congestion in the cities, air pollution, the depletion of fossil fuels.

As BC Transit prepares to meet these challenges with convenient rapid transit systems to the suburbs and clean-running, fuel efficient vehicles, it takes advantage of the experience of its predecessors, and 100 years of public transit in the province.

The busy corner of Main and Hastings in downtown Vancouver, ca. 1918. The Carnegie Library is on the left, and the large, three-sectioned Ford Building is on the right. Like today, public transit had enormous influence on the business and social life of the city.

APPENDIX

TRANSIT SYSTEMS IN BRITISH COLUMBIA

Prior to the 1970s, transit systems in British Columbia outside Greater Victoria and Greater Vancouver were operated privately, or by the municipalities themselves, without the benefit of provincial funding. In 1972 the province began to offer funding to the smaller communities, and between 1972 and 1978 a variety of provincial funding arrangements were available. The following communities took advantage of them during this period:

City of Kamloops	1975	City of Nelson	1972
City of Kelowna	1974	City of Penticton	1977
District of Kitimat	1974	City of Port Alberni	1975
Regional District of Kootenay-		District of Powell River	1972
Boundary	1977	City of Prince George	1975
District of Maple Ridge	1976	City of Prince Rupert	1975
Regional District of Nanaimo	1972		

Following the Urban Transit Authority Act of July 1978, many more communities came under the new comprehensive funding program.

1979	April 1	District of Mission	conventional buses
	November 1	Regional District of Okanagan Similkimeen	Paratransit
1980	June 1	District of Chilliwack	conventional buses
	August 18	City of Terrace	conventional buses
	August 18	City of Vernon	conventional buses
1981	January 2	City of Kelowna	handyDART
	January 15	City of Fort St. John	conventional buses
	March 2	Regional District of Central Okanagan	conventional buses
	April 1	District of Coldstream	conventional buses
	April 1	City of Dawson Creek	conventional buses
	April 1	City of Prince George	handyDART
	May 1	City of Kamloops	handyDART
	August 1	Town of Comox	Paratransit
1982	January 1	City of Cranbrook	Paratransit
	January 1	City of Kimberley	Paratransit
	January 1	Regional District of Sunshine Coast	Paratransit
	January 1	City of Williams Lake	Paratransit
	January 4	District of Campbell River	Paratransit
	February 2	City of Vernon	handyDART
	April 1	Regional District of Central Kootenay (Nelson)	Paratransit
	April 1	District of Maple Ridge	handyDART
	April 1	City of Penticton	handyDART
	April 1	Town of Princeton	Paratransit
	April 1	City of Quesnel	Paratransit
	April 1	District of Summerland	Paratransit
	July 1	District of Abbotsford	handyDART
	July 1	District of Matsqui	handyDART
	October 1	Regional District of Alberni Clayoquot	handyDART

1986	July 15	City of Prince Rupert	handyDART
	August 28	District of Abbotsford	conventional buses
	August 28	District of Matsqui	conventional buses
	November 28	Regional District of Central Kootenay (Castlegar)	conventional buses
1987	May 25	District of North Cowichan	Paratransit
	May 25	City of Duncan	Paratransit
1989	April 3	Regional District of Central Kootenay (Creston)	Paratransit
	April 24	Regional District of Nanaimo	handyDART
	June	Regional District of Central Kootenay (Castlegar)	handyDART
	June 26	District of Chilliwack	handyDART
	July 31	Regional District of Central Kootenay (Nakusp)	Paratransit
	November 20	Regional District of Kootenay Boundary	handyDART

INDEX

ILLUSTRATION CREDITS

The authors thank the following individuals and institutions for making photographs available. References are to page number and position of the illustration on the page. BC Hydro 10a, 12a, 18b, 20a, 21b, 22a/c, 23a, 32b, 41b, 54a, 55b, 67a, 73, 77a, 80, 83b, 86a, 113a, 147; BC Transit 6, 12b, 17a, 22b, 24b, 32a, 33a/b, 36a, 38a–d, 42a/b, 44c, 45, 50, 54b, 59a/b, 64, 65a, 68a, 69a, 74a, 75a/b, 77b, 78, 81a/b, 82b, 83a, 84–85, 87c, 88a/b, 92a/b, 94a, 95, 100a/b, 101a/b, 102a/b, 103a/b, 104–105, 106b, 108a/b, 109, 110b, 111a/b, 112a/b, 114b, 115a/b, 118a/b, 119a/b, 120, 121a/b, 122a, 123a, 124, 127, 128a/b, 129a–c, 130a/b, 131, 132a–c, 133a/b, 134, 135a/b, 136, 137a/b, 138–139, 140a/b, 141a/b, 142, 143a/b, 144a–c, 145a/b, 146; Bill Boston 65b; Chilliwack Museum 60b; Ted Clark 28b, 89b; R. Corley 49a; Miles Cornborough 27, 97; Peter Cox 87a, 89d; Norm Gidney 91a; Ken Hodgson i, 1, 39b, 40a, 66, 74b; Bruce Holcomb 37b; Irving House Museum 48b; Brian Kelly Collection 2, 28c, 30a/b, 34–35, 36b, 39a, 41a, 44b, 46, 51a, 52, 53a/b, 56–57, 58a, 61, 82a, 86b, 87b, 89c, 90, 91b, 93a/b, 96, 98–99, 106a, 107, 114a, 122b, 126a; Langley Centennial Museum 60a; M.D. McCarter 37a; Robert McVay 62–63; Mission Museum 68b, 72a; New Westminster Public Library 51b, 116–117; North Shore Museum 29b, 31a/b, 113, 126b; North Shore News 94b; Ernie Plant 72b, 76, 89a, 101c; Provincial Archives of British Columbia 5, 8, 10b, 11, 13a, 14–15, 16a/b, 19, 29a, 48a, 70–71; Richmond Museum and Archives 58b; Barry Sanford 110a; Vic Sharman 44a; Vancouver City Archives 13b, 18a, 28a, 49b, 55a; Vancouver Island Coach Lines 123b; Vancouver Public Library 26; Victoria City Archives 17b, 20b, 21a, 24a; Bob Webster 23b; W. Whittaker 43a; W.H. Young 92c. Maps drawn by Theresa Magee.

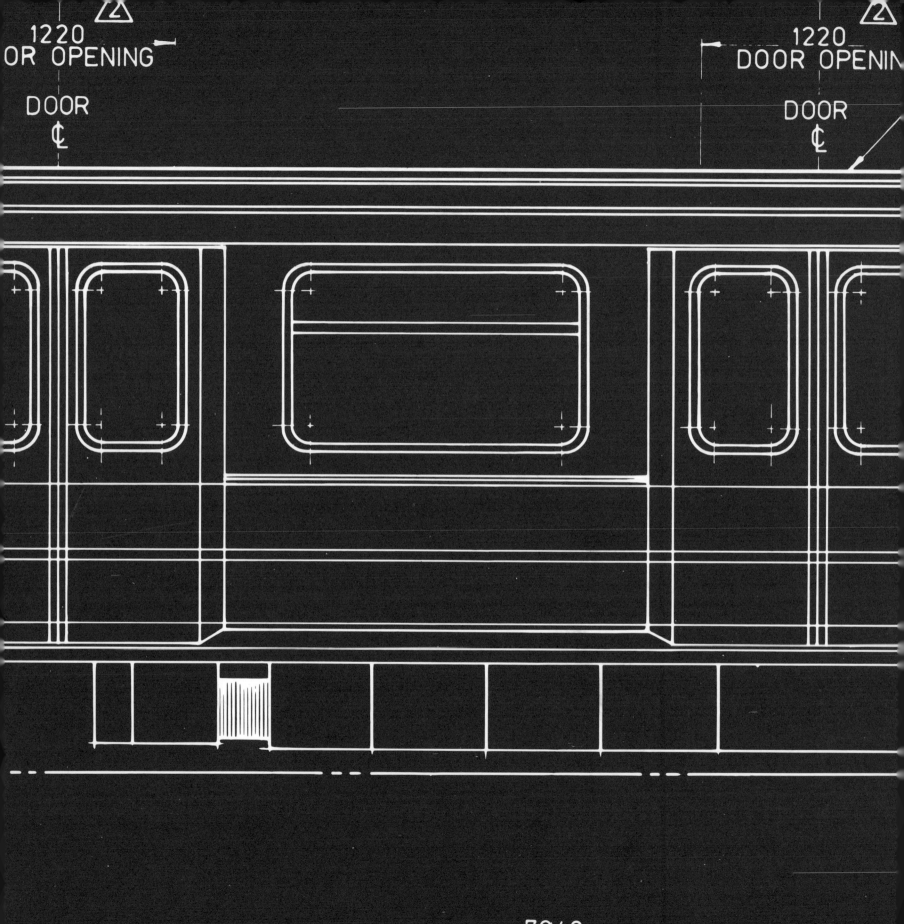

7940